JACKSON'S TRACK
REVISITED

HISTORY, REMEMBRANCE AND RECONCILIATION

CAROLYN LANDON

MONASH
UNIVERSITY
PUBLISHING

DEDICATION

To Daryl Tonkin, Bushman

ACKNOWLEDGEMENTS

Thank you to Barbara Caine and Maria Nugent for your foresight in recognising the importance of further exploration of Daryl Tonkin's story and encouraging me to go ahead with this project.

Thank you to Janet Cowden for revealing your father's papers and leading me into the Archive.

Thank you to the members of the Warragul Historical Society for generously opening your archive to me.

Thank you, especially, to Margaret Batten, for your lively and intelligent interest, your constant help and encouragement.

Finally, thank you to my valued friend, Pauline Mullett: your energy and sense of purpose have inspired me throughout the writing of this book.

JACKSON'S TRACK REVISITED

HISTORY, REMEMBRANCE AND RECONCILIATION

CONTENTS

○ A NOTE ABOUT PAGINATION AND CHAPTER IDENTIFICATION

Page numbers in this book do not run consecutively across chapters. Instead, page numbering restarts on the first page of each chapter and is prefaced by the chapter number. Thus, 01.1 is chapter one, page one; 01.2 is chapter one, page two. 02.1 is chapter two, page one; 02.2 is chapter two, page two, and so on.

As page numbering restarts at the beginning of each chapter, page numbers are not listed in the Table of Contents.

This system, in which page numbering is self-contained within each chapter, allows the publisher, Monash University ePress, to publish individual chapters online.

○ PREFACE

In 1999, as the co-author of *Jackson's Track: Memoir of a Dreamtime Place*, Carolyn Landon helped to produce the riveting and moving story of Daryl Tonkin's life amidst the Aboriginal community that settled around his Gippsland timber works. After spending a great deal of time talking to Tonkin, Landon wrote up his story, representing as closely as possible his point of view in his own voice. Inevitably she shaped the story, but she saw herself essentially as listener and facilitator, enabling Tonkin to tell the story of his early family life; his marriage to Euphemia Hood Mullett, a woman of the Brabralung Clan of the Kurnai Tribe; and his life with their children and the Aboriginal community that settled around his timber works and worked with him. *Jackson's Track* also told of the tragic demise and destruction of this community after Euphemia's death. The acclaim that *Jackson's Track* received on its publication showed not only how important this story was, but also how prescient Landon had been in bringing it to light in the memoir form, which gave it authenticity and pathos.

In the years since the publication of *Jackson's Track,* through her growing knowledge of the local area and community and her interest and involvement in the reconciliation movement, Landon has come to see that Tonkin's story was not the only possible version. The stories of others involved raised questions that Tonkin never addressed, as well as offering very different accounts of the players and their communities. In one way then *Jackson's Track Revisited* brings to the fore these other recollections and memories, enabling one to see clearly the many different interests, concerns and experiences that make up the whole story of Jackson's Track throughout the 1940s, '50s and '60s. But Landon also revisits Tonkin's own memories and her own approach to his story, reflecting on her assumptions about the nature of history and biography.

Jackson's Track Revisited offers wonderful insights into the differences between memory and the formal historical record, the history that is found in documents used to formulate policy and record the official version of events. Landon's depiction of the difficulties involved in bringing together these two forms of history is not only fascinating, but also raises many questions about how accurately the lives of indigenous peoples can be known or understood if one relies only on the written record.

The stories in this new work are every bit as compelling as was that of Daryl Tonkin. They are augmented by the powerful voice of Landon herself, reflecting on and explaining how she came to record, analyse and understand anew the history of Jackson's Track.

Barbara Caine, School of Historical Studies, Monash University, May 2006

'It is our failure to imagine these things being done to us. With some noble exceptions, we failed to make the most basic human response and enter into their hearts and minds.'

Don Watson
Redfern Speech spoken by Paul Keating, 1992

'The most courageous characters are those with imagination, those who, through their imaginative faculty, can empathise with others. When you lack this kind of courage, you remain ignorant of others' feelings and needs.'

Azar Nafisi, *Reading Lolita in Tehran* (2003, Random House)

'What I want to do,' I said, surprising myself, for until that moment I had not managed to articulate it, even in my thoughts, 'is to enlarge my imagination to the point where it can encompass truths as widely separated as your version of events and the Cinques'.'

Helen Garner, *Joe Cinque's Consolation* (2004, Pan McMillan)

○ THE STORIES

Carolyn Landon

Jackson's Track Revisited delves into the story told by Daryl Tonkin in *Jackson's Track* (Penguin, Australia, 2000) of his life in the great Gippsland forest living among Aboriginal timber workers. Just as his family has hoped, Daryl Tonkin's story has created the space for more stories to come. These include remembered stories from Aboriginal people and the White Australians who were entangled with them in the 1950s, the era of assimilation. They also include traces of story thrown up by 'the Archive' and local historical society collections. An exploration of the historical factors surrounding Daryl's memoir leads to discussion of the Victorian Welfare Board, the Victorian Aborigines' Advancement League and the policy of assimilation that was so prevalent in the mid-twentieth century in Australia. Daryl's story enters the realm of History.

Daryl's house
Photo by Julian Hills

Imagine a shack that looks more like a pile of weather beaten timber than a standing construction. It is in the middle of a windswept paddock on the edge of the great Gippsland State Forest, which sweeps down from the Baw Baw Ranges. Imagine that inside this building two people sit at a cleared table that is covered with clean newspaper.

One of them, a bushman of eighty years who would rather be outside on such a good day, is talking, and the other, a woman half his age, is listening and writing. They are oblivious to the wind and the weather, to flies buzzing round their heads, and to snakes and rodents lurking about the house. Together they are writing down a story that will change the lives of many people in their local community and the minds of many more people in the greater Australian community.

Daryl and Carolyn at Daryl's house
Photo by Ingvar Kenne, © 2003

It is March 1996. The old man in this picture is Daryl Tonkin and I am the woman who is drawing a story out of him with careful questions, taking notes while he talks. Later I will shape the old man's memories into an accessible 'yarn' that I will read out to him at the beginning of our next session. During the eighteen months that this process lasts, the old man tells his version of events that he remembers happening between 1937 and 1962 in what I identify as the era of assimilation. It is the story of his life at Jackson's Track, where he and his brother owned a timber mill and 880 acres of forest. For over twenty years, people, mostly Aboriginal people from Lake Tyers, came to live and work there. It was at Jackson's Track that Daryl met and 'married' Euphemia Hood, a 'full-blood' Kurnai woman, and lived with her and their children for most of the rest of his life. It is a story of hard work, happiness, betrayal, racial prejudice, false assumptions and, ultimately, in Daryl's view, tragic dispossession. Under my influence Daryl's story becomes a life story in the Augustinian sense, written *'pro vita sua* (that is, as a defence of one's own life)'[1] and it is plotted as a classic tale with beginning, middle and end – ascending action, climax and denouement. It is published in 1999 as *Jackson's Track: Memoir of a Dreamtime place* and is received by a wide readership in the Australian community.[2]

That was six years ago. Daryl Tonkin and I would never have met, nor would his memoir ever have been written, were it not for his daughter, Pauline Mullett. Although her father is Anglo-Australian, Pauline's identity lies with her mother, Euphemia Hood Mullett, a woman of the Brabralung Clan of the Kurnai Tribe.[3] Euphemia handed down to her precocious daughter the knowledge of tribal culture that her own father, Stewart Hood, had handed down to her. Stewart's knowledge, in turn, had come from his grandmother, Kitty Perry Johnson, one of the 'old people' who remembered back before white settlement. Pauline understood the cultural importance of keeping her mother's knowledge and eventually handing it down to her own daughter when the time came. However, she was also curious about the recent 'history' of Jackson's Track, a tract of country in the foothills of the Baw Baw Ranges in West Gippsland, deeply forested with giant mountain ash, silver top, and stringy bark and covered with the pink and white blooms of boronia each spring. It was there that Pauline had grown up with her eleven brothers and sisters. The sound of saws whining at the mill and of axes ringing in the bush were a constant part of Pauline's life as a small child, but she had been born too late to remember the place at the time when her extended family also lived there, when it had been a thriving community of 'blackfellas' all of whose livelihoods depended on the timber mill run by her father and his brother. She knew that only her father could tell her about his life there and about events that occurred before she was born, events about which she had heard rumours all her life. She wanted to know that story so she could hand it down to her own children and tell it to others in her community. She also suspected that the wider community might be ready to hear these stories, that it might be the right time to give recognition to a whole group of Aboriginal people whose history was part of West Gippsland. And so she asked her father to tell his story.

Reluctantly, the old man sat down with ball-point pen and a pad of lined A4 paper he'd bought at the news agent and began to pull his memories together into a narrative of life in the timber mills on Jackson's Track. After he had completed twenty-five pages, he considered the task done and gave what he had written to Pauline, who was eagerly awaiting his chronicle. As she read the pages, however, it became obvious that the old man had left most of the 'history' she was looking for out of his story and she was momentarily stymied.

At that time, I was a secondary school English teacher at one of the schools where Pauline was Koori Educator. I was not only a colleague but also taught two of her children, and so a tentative but ultimately enduring friendship developed between us. When Pauline realised she needed help to goad her father into telling his stories, it was natural that she would call on me. She told me what she wanted, handed me her father's handwritten manuscript, and left me to decide what I would do.

I read the pages with some trepidation, for as I deciphered her father's old fashioned copperplate hand on that flimsy paper I felt I was being asked to look over something quaint and steeped in the kind of old clichés of Australian bush life that settler Australians – at least those who still live in the bush – are weened on. Here were mostly campfire yarns about the heroics and foolhardiness of the characters involved in the timber industry in West Gippsland. I assumed he knew a great deal more than he wrote since Pauline was so anxious for his story to be told, but it occurred to me that these might be the only stories the old man knew how to tell. It was hard to take his pages seriously. Out of respect for Pauline I read on until, at last, I came upon a key passage Daryl had slipped in at the very end of his narrative:

> A group of Christians [who] were white people didn't understand blackfellows [sic] ways and bush living. They dogged the blacks for years trying to change their ways and give up the bush... They held a meeting in Drouin and decided to separate the blacks away from each other and the only way was to move them away from the bush and to destroy their homes then take them away in trucks and separate them away from each other in different towns... So they came out to Jackson's Track and went around the homes telling them what was decided for them. The blacks said they would not shift away from their homes but were told the bulldozer was coming to push their homes down and would be burnt. They were told to gather up their belongings or they would be burnt. The bulldozer arrived with the

trucks and pushed all the houses down then put a match to them. The blacks were told to get on the trucks and were taken to the block of land near Drouin... The Christians had wrecked the blackfellows lifes [*sic*]... They drowned their sorrows in drink which affected their health and they died one after another.[4]

This unsentimental and concise description of a tragedy convinced me to spend as much energy as it might take to help Pauline with her father's story. It was clear that if we could get Daryl Tonkin to talk, every word would be worth listening to. This passage became the centre of all my questioning and continued to drive my curiosity as Daryl's story widened, and expanded to other participants in events he finally related to me. From the moment I read that passage, I found my life deeply entangled with Pauline's life, that of her father and with the lives of those, far and wide, connected with his story.

As soon as Daryl and I began to work together it was evident, from his reluctance and his occasional tears, that the process of drawing out the old man's story was laden with pain and danger for him. Ever since he had fallen in love with and begun to live with an Aboriginal woman back in the late 1940s, Daryl had kept details of his life private and hidden. From that time on, his instinct had been to camouflage himself in order to remain invisible to his European compatriots, as his new extended family had always been forced to do. Consequently, I found working with this old man fraught with difficulty. It seemed that after almost forty years of keeping quiet about so many things in his life, the task of telling his story was almost overwhelming. But Pauline's encouragement and strength of purpose gave him courage, and he found a way to answer my questions until a narrative was formed and the book was made.

As Daryl's story took shape, I began to realise what Pauline already knew: that something bigger than all of us was evolving. But of the three of us bound together by this project, only I was concerned that we were standing, like three innocents in an epic tale, at the portals of a huge Victorian edifice called History. In my mind it was akin to the Victorian Parliament looming at the top end of Bourke Street in Melbourne with broad stone stairs, Doric columns and many tall doors with heavy, brass fittings leading to a labyrinth inside. The edifice was hallowed and sacred, yet political and profane. The door we were entering was called Memoir, a portal that led the uninitiated into a hall of mirrors where it is difficult to tell truth from fiction. We were naïve enough to be ignorant of the complexity of the path we were taking and so, ignoring the switchbacks, false lanes, steep ascents and treacherous curves, we stumbled on – telling, listening, questioning, writing – until a manuscript was completed and a book was published.

If I had had a better idea of what it meant, in terms of historiography and methodo-logy, to enter the labyrinth, I might have been overwhelmed and called a halt. Thank goodness for my naïveté. Daryl was even more naïve than I. In his mind, if he thought of it at all, the edifice we were entering must have seemed a simple structure built by simple truths. He indicated time and time again that he was telling the 'true story of Jackson's Track' once and for all. Nothing could have been further from the truth.

Pauline's vision of our project was different again. It didn't take me long to realise that she did not see a Victorian edifice, as I did; that her idea of history was much more fluid than mine. At first, rather than pay attention to her ideas, I remained comfortable with my own limited assumptions. I was slow to understand that she was wary of how I was going about the project, that my unconsciously Western way of thinking about story – especially 'life story', which in the European tradition is 'no natural or eternal form'[5] as I then thought it was – was clashing with things she knew about history, identification, family, story telling and song. To her there was no edifice that could hold these things. She watched me closely, and slowly, slowly she brought me towards an understanding of a way of being and a kind of knowledge that most White Australians know little about.

As a migrant to Australia in 1968, I thought I would find Aboriginal people to be part of the mix of the culture in Victoria, the state in which I live. Instead, all I found was a blank space and little interest in Aboriginal culture or pre-history from the settler Australians around me. The first thing I was told was that there were no 'full-blood' Aborigines left in Victoria, that they were a dying race, that their culture was extinct. In rural Victoria, these beliefs prevail and in the early 1990s, when I began to enter Pauline's world, there was very little evidence to the contrary. While an indigenous presence in popular Australian culture was emerging, none of it seemed to be Victorian. It turned out that for more than three generations, very few of us had been paying serious attention to Pauline's world.[6] Through her father's story, Pauline hoped – perhaps subconsciously, at that moment she impulsively asked him to tell it – to lay the groundwork for a new awareness of her culture. She hoped that its complex hierarchies, cultural imperatives, traditional assumptions – as labyrinthine to her as that Victorian edifice called History was to me – would be revealed as another way of seeing. Her instincts told her that in the 1990s, with the reconciliation movement on the way, White Australian society might be ready to learn her way of seeing. I was her tool. She was hoping that more stories, the hidden stories of her people – stories from her mother and aunty in particular – would follow her father's memoir as part of this process.

Pauline
Photo by Ingvar Kenne, © 2003

It came about that once the book was published, Pauline's hopes began to materialise. It seemed as though almost everyone in the Warragul-Drouin district, where Daryl lived and where the story of *Jackson's Track* took place, read the book and spoke about it to one another.[7] Because the book revealed a happy, independent and active Aboriginal community, it pushed local people's imagination to the brink. First the local newspaper proclaimed its shock that an Aboriginal community such as the one Daryl had described existed at all. Then, in another issue of the paper, local historian John Wells confessed at length that he had been caught unawares. The book forced local people to think about the make-up of their community and to confront their assumptions about the Aboriginal people who, unbeknown to many, lived amongst them. It created an atmosphere of acceptance and a new curiosity. It also seemed to give the Kurnai people the confidence to emerge from the shadows in which they had been living for more than forty years and begin, tentatively, to take their place in the community. The book's popularity among Australian readers gave Daryl's life story a kind of celebrity status and a legitimacy that enabled citizens in the wider Gippsland area to change the vision they had of their community. As Michael Frisch expressed it in an essay on his experiences of the impact of oral history, Daryl's story forced the citizens to 're-imagine how the past connects with the present and the possibilities this vantage suggests for the future'.[8] Just as Pauline had hoped, her father's story seemed to create the space for more stories to follow.

Pauline was more concerned with the stories of her own people than of those of the citizens of Daryl's generation who took part in and were, according to him, responsible for the tragic events he related at the end of his book. Over the eighteen months that Daryl and I worked together, Pauline and I had become increasingly aware that his memoir was only one version of events. I had come to realise that it was not the 'history' he proclaimed it to be, but merely an example of a new kind of engagement with history that was gaining momentum and had, over the last twenty years, challenged many of the assumptions of conventional scholarship. It was the kind of history that comes 'from the bottom up and from the outside in to challenge the established organisation of knowledge and power and politics that rest on it'.[9] For this reason, while Pauline was waiting for her people to find the courage to speak up, I was waiting for the pillars of our community to begin screaming foul play at how Daryl – and by association I – may have perverted the facts to serve our own ends. However, the popularity of *Jackson's Track*, and the fact that it was a story of tragedy and reproach, left those citizens still living who may have taken part in some of the events Daryl recounted – people who had served on the shire council, had been policemen, welfare workers or evangelists – unwilling, at first, to speak out. Nevertheless, I waited, knowing that one day someone would say something.

And finally this happened. In 2002, through the Reconciliation Group in Warragul, I came to know Janet Cowden. Because she was such a quiet, seemingly timid woman, who rarely spoke, it was almost a year of attending meetings with her before I really began to notice her. She dressed in a fairly conservative manner, as if to divert attention from herself. At the meetings she sat with a straight, self-contained posture, taking notes, but in writing so small it was impossible for a curious person to sneak a look at the words she wrote. Some of us wondered why she came to the meetings and what she could possibly be gaining from the process.

For some months in a row Janet brought along to the meetings a large cloth bag with something heavy in it, leaving it unopened each time. Finally, at the last meeting of the year, she sat directly across from me at a small table and, as proceedings began, she took a very old cardboard box with a lid on it out of the bag and carefully placed it in front of her on the table. She must have had some purpose in doing this, but she did not look up to give us a chance to ask her about it. I was intrigued. Finally, as the meeting drew to a close and people were leaving, I could contain my curiosity no longer. I asked Janet what was in the box. People paused to see what she would say. She seemed to blush deeply when my attention centred on her, but she summoned up enough courage to take the lid off and show the group the contents. She carefully began to explain that her father had been the secretary or treasurer, possibly both, of the local branch of the Victorian Aborigines Advancement League. Those who were still at the meeting returned to their seats.

Janet handed me a piece of paper that had, in carefully inked columns – blue ink penned with a fine nib on yellowing, lined paper – a list of the members of the Neerim branch of the Victorian Aborigines Advancement League. Even before I passed it on to others, I realised I was looking at something vitally important to Daryl's story. I recognised many names on the list. Some were from well-known local families and all were Anglo-Australian names (with the exception of one Dutch name). There were no local Aboriginal names that I could see. At first I thought that the list might be non-denominational – indeed even secular – because it included the name of a now retired local doctor known for his left-wing ideas. But when Janet pulled out the minutes of the branch meetings it became clear there was a strong Christian flavour to the proceedings. Janet said her father was deeply religious, as was she.

At that point, I had no clear idea of what the Victorian Aborigines Advancement League was. The word League was dated and quaint to my ears. But I was fully aware that foremost among the names on the list were all the people Daryl Tonkin had called 'the do-gooders' in *Jackson's Track* – those he had described in his hand-written notes as 'Christians [who] had wrecked the blackfellows [*sic*] lives'. I was certain Janet knew what I knew and I wondered if she could sense my excitement. She dug into the box to show us that she had in her possession correspondence, treasurer's reports, receipts, and some of the minutes of the Neerim Branch of the Aborigines Advancement League throughout the mid-1950s to the late 1960s. My eyes widened. These were exactly the years most discussed in Daryl's memoir. It turned out that Janet had worked for many years for the Summer Institute of Linguistics in Darwin as an archivist, and so she was fully aware of the uses to which her documents could be put. Indeed, if she hadn't the habits of an archivist, she may have burned the lot long ago. As it was, she had systematically gone through her parents' papers after her father had died, sorted them and recorded them for posterity. Now that they were open before us and it was obvious that

Janet Cowden during her career as an archivist
Photo courtesy Janet Cowden

they were intimately connected to Daryl's life, she must have felt it was a confirmation of her effort.

Others at the table were interested in the papers, but they seemed not to be aware of their significance. They began to make moves to leave, but I remained in my seat, as did Janet and another woman, Margaret Batten. As the night wore on, the three of us scrutinised the contents of the box thoroughly. Finally, Janet carefully began to gather up the documents and return them to the box. But before she replaced the lid, she gave me permission to use the material to find out as much as I could about the League, the history, and her father's part in it.

"Yes," she said to me when I asked if she would be willing to open up and let her father's side of the story be told. "My family is willing to be exposed in that way."

The word *exposed* revealed what an act of courage it was for her to let me see the contents of the box. It indicated how sensitive I would have to be with her and her family as a listener/researcher. If the process turned out to be at all confronting or uncomfortable, she, unlike Daryl, might cut and run. I expressed my gratitude to her, telling her I thought she was helping to open up the way for other stories to be told at last, stories from people such as her father Hector Cowden (as remembered by his daughter Flo Cowden White, Janet's younger sister who remembers the Track better than she does), and from Alwyn Jensen, another very active member of the League who spent much time and energy with the people at Jackson's Track and who, Janet informed me, is still alive and waiting to reveal his version of events.

In turn, Pauline informed me that new information would be coming to light from her Aunty Gina Rose, her mother's sister, who was willing to tell her version of the story. Aunty Gina is a respected Kurnai Elder and remembers living at the Track and the League's involvement in her move away from it. Dot Mullett, Murray Austin and Gary (Chock) Mullett, all of whom grew up at the Track and moved off it into the town with their parents, were also willing to tell what they remembered. These new versions would stretch out Daryl's story, add new dimensions, possibly even conflict with his memories of what happened for they would be told from different points of view. They would add texture to the story already told and give us an even more dynamic sense of what it might have been like to be at Jackson's Track in the late 1950s.

Janet's box of papers is also a reminder that there are other sources of story besides memory. When Janet let me handle the fragile documents she had preserved, they seemed to my Europeanised mind to be History, real History, in the way that over the last two hundred years or so, records like these have been considered by traditional historians to be the only valid source of history. Records like these are usually found in the archive and they have a certain smell: a smell of age, of artefact, of proof. *Dust* is what Carolyn Steedman calls this smell. It is this *Dust* that triggers excitement and anticipation, that can give the researcher fever – archive fever.[10] And indeed, these documents did make me tremble. They were imbued with the thoughts, activities, aspirations and good and tragic deeds of a group of people I had already met through Daryl's story but heretofore had no access to. When I read some of the letters in Janet's box that were hand-written by Alwyn Jensen to various people, it occurred to me that he never intended that someone like me would have access to his papers. In fact, later on when I met and told him what I had seen, he was quite surprised that those letters still existed. Nevertheless I could not tell how he felt about my having handled them and read them. If he were shocked or experienced it as an invasion, he kept it to himself. There were more letters by Hector Cowden about the appalling conditions at the Track, about the kindness of Mrs Buchanan (another member of the League mentioned in Daryl's story) in supplying clothing and shoes to the 'fringe dwellers', about the apathy of the Welfare Board in giving any assistance, and about the wrong-mindedness of Board policy. These documents reveal a point of view so different to Daryl's that, although they talk about the same time, the same place and the same people, the writers might as well have been writing about events on a different planet. Janet's box made me understand that I would have to enter the Archive to find enough traces from the past to piece together these other stories. This was the only way I could satisfy myself that I had found enough and heard enough to round out Daryl's story to a satisfactory level for Pauline and me.

What follows is a journey through all the stories Pauline and I could lay our hands on. It is also an account of our own journeys towards some kind of understanding of the past, the present, ourselves and each other. All the stories must be heard and considered together, for each one complements the others, making up a dynamic and satisfying whole. But, I am also mindful the last story will merely have laid the groundwork for more stories. And there will be stories to come; there is no last word.

ENDNOTES

1
    Sansom (2001).

2
    Jackson's Track: Memoir of a Dreamtime place by Carolyn Landon and Daryl Tonkin (Landon and Tonkin 1999) was published by Penguin in Melbourne 1999; it won the Victorian Community History Award 2000, Australian Human Rights Award 2000; short listed for NSW and Queensland Premier's Literary Awards 2000; it has been on the Schools Senior English list and has become a staple of Penguin's back list.

3
    The spellings come from *The native tribes of South-East Australia* (Howitt 2001, p. 272).

4
    Landon and Tonkin (1999, pp. 24–25)

5
    (Sansom 2001, pp. 99).

6
    Historians Bain Attwood and Jan Critchett and anthropologist Diane Barwick, among others, were writing about Victorian Aboriginal people in the 1970s and 80s, but their work at that time was largely focused on the 19th Century. Only lately has that focus changed to the present. In the 1940s and 50s, influential anthropologists, A. P. Elkin and D. Thompson, put forward the theory that, due to contact with settler Australians, South Eastern Aboriginal people had lost all their cultural practices by the beginning of the 20th century.

[7] The Penguin sales records for *Jackson's Track* (Landon and Tonkin 1999) show a huge spike in the Warragul-Drouin area specifically and then the whole of Gippsland more generally, as well as hefty sales throughout Australia: approximately 60,000 books to date. The story has been well-publicised in local papers with long and prominent feature articles by Carolyn Turner and John Wells. Every service group, book club, library and school in Warragul-Drouin area has requested talks by the author(s).

[8] Frisch (1989, p. xvii).

[9] Frisch (1989, p. xvii).

[10] Steedman (2001, p. 9).

REFERENCES

Frisch, Michael. 1989. *Shared authority: Essays on the craft and meaning of oral and public history*. New York: University of New York.

Howitt, A. W. 2001. *The native tribes of South-East Australia, facsimile edition of book first published in 1904*. Canberra: Aboriginal Studies Press.

Landon, Carolyn; Tonkin, Daryl. 1999. *Jackson's Track: Memoir of a Dreamtime place*. Melbourne: Penguin.

Sansom, Basil. 2001. 'In the absence of vita as genre: The making of the Roy Kelly story'. In *Telling stories: Indigenous history and memory in Australia and New Zealand*, edited by Attwood, Bain; Magowan, Fiona. Sydney: Allen & Unwin.

Steedman, Carolyn. 2001. *Dust*. Manchester: Manchester University Press.

Cite this chapter as: Landon, Carolyn. 2006. 'The stories'. In *Jackson's Track revisited: History, remembrance and reconciliation*. Melbourne: Monash University ePress. pp. 1.1–1.13. DOI: 10.2104/jtr06001.

CHAPTER 2

THE STORY IN THE ARCHIVE

Carolyn Landon

This chapter explores the idea of 'The Archive' as a repository for stories. Once it was a place for only a select few, those deemed worthy and capable of interpreting the documents in the archive and of wielding their power. Now there is an attempt to make the Archive accessible to all. Despite this, it retains for those who enter a feeling of 'History' – History in the traditional sense of something linear, positivist and patriarchal, as if one could follow a clue and find a true answer to any question. It is a feeling of something created by men for men who rule. The historian sorts through documents pertaining to the subject: letters, memos, complaints, minutes, bills of sale, titles, lists and more lists. Who would have thought so much would have been saved? Yet, although all the documents deal with Aboriginal affairs, they contain no Aboriginal voices. The attitudes in the documents represent the status quo, albeit in changing contexts.

I enter the Archive for the first time in my life in 2002. Janet Cowden has told me that her opinionated father was a great letter writer. She is sure he wrote letters to the editor of the local paper more than once. I have decided to search through the papers held by the Warragul Historical Society to see if I can find further traces of Hector Cowden. I believe that they will lead into the Jackson's Track story along a path completely different from the one Daryl Tonkin followed. The historical moment has changed and become more complex and more interesting than it was when I first met Daryl in 1996. Now, those of us who are attempting to expand our imaginations to encompass new and divergent viewpoints are greatly challenged. Not only are we trying to meet the challenge of opening our minds to the Aboriginal points of view, but we are also being goaded into a new consideration of the views of those settler Australians who dealt with and made policy for Aboriginal people in the past. I am being guided in this second direction in particular by the Victorian Aboriginal Advancement League documents that Janet has shown me. And so I find myself entering the Historical labyrinth through a new door called Archive but this time I am fully aware of its complexity as I had not been when I entered the Memoir portal.

The Warragul Historical Society is situated in the original Warragul Shire offices.[1] The building is a small jewel of Victorian architecture made of brick and stone with a portico sheltering great heavy doors. Inside, a wide corridor under a lofty ceiling leads past more heavy doors behind which are beautiful rooms with great high windows surrounded by ornate architraves. At the end of the corridor a grand staircase is lit by crystal covered lamps hanging down on long brass chains. Upstairs in the old Council Chamber, empty and full of shadows, there is a feeling of ghosts lurking. Perhaps they are maintaining witness. Despite large windows, the light inside the reading room on the first floor is very dim in the late afternoons. Motes of dust dance in the thin beams of cold light entering through the wavy window glass. The dust rises up from volumes of local newspapers going back as far as 1880.

Dust! I think. This is the place where I will find History.

I am allowed to search through and view the yellowing flaking papers. I look for traces of Hector Cowden but the first thing I see is a reference to the local Aborigines Advancement League back in 1958. My eyes alight on the headline 'District League Has Done Much to Advance Welfare of Aborigines'.[2] My heartbeat quickens and I can hardly keep from calling out 'Eureka!' I return to this old building and sit alone or with Janet and Margaret Batten, week after week until our discoveries there lead to the Victorian Public Records Office and the National Australian Archive. In those places I sort through all sorts of documents pertaining to my subject – letters, memos, complaints, minutes, bills of sale, titles, lists and more lists. Who would have thought so much would have been saved? The imagination, excited by 'archive fever', careens into the bowels of the Archive conjuring miles and miles of shelves lined with traces of more facets of human endeavour than one could imagine.

Janet Cowden
Photo courtesy of the Cowden family

The Archive is a repository for stories. Its ledgers, letters, registers, reports, minutes, memos and articles all contain stories and are the stuff from which stories can be made. Derrida writes of it as 'the place where things begin, where power originates, its workings inextricably bound up with the authority of beginnings...'[3] Once it was a place for only a select few, those deemed worthy and capable of interpreting the documents in the Archive and of wielding their power. Now there is an attempt to make the Archive accessible to all. However, it is still only the educated – the researcher, historian or writer – who venture in to interpret the meaning of the treasure in the Archive. When one enters, no matter how modern a building it might be, there is a feeling of History – History in the traditional sense of something linear, positivist and patriarchal, as if one could follow a clue and find a true answer to any question. In other words, there is a feeling of something created by men for men who rule. All the documents placed on my table by the archivist at the brand new Victorian Public Records Office in North Melbourne were written by men for men, as were all the documents in Janet's box, and the newspaper articles I locate in the Historical Society. It seems to me, from the wording of the documents they wrote, that these men were all articulating the dominant culture – Eurocentric and therefore civilised, socially and culturally androcentric, spiritually and racially superior – in which most of them felt secure and complacent. Although the documents I read deal with Aboriginal affairs, they contain no Aboriginal voices, with one exception: a report in the local newspaper that included a direct quote from Doug Nicholls, who, at the time the article was written, was a local Aboriginal pastor. The attitudes in the documents represented the status quo, albeit in changing contexts.

As a result of my frustrating experience looking for an Aboriginal voice in the Archive, I come to understand that it stands for what can and cannot be said, written or read. As early as the 1960s, Michel Foucault wrote in *The archaeology of knowledge* that the Archive *is* the 'system that establishes statements as events and things'.[4] This makes it a symbol of power, a metaphor for the processes of collecting traces of the past, of deciding what gets recorded, what gets used and what gets lost. The Archive seems so immediate and intimate that a researcher can be swayed and overcome by the points of view expressed in the documents. No matter how coldly they are written, we see personality, relationships, assumptions, attitudes, even desires and failures in them. It seems to me that it is this intimacy that gives the researcher 'archive fever', and we must guard against it. The only way to stay healthy is to measure the Story from the Archive against the stories gathered from the memories of those who were witnesses and draw conclusions that can lead to new ways of seeing the past, present and future.

For me, the particular story that the Archive throws up, as if out of the ether, stretches out Daryl Tonkin's memoir immeasurably. His narrative, since it is a memoir, is, according to Carolyn Steedman, a variant of the novel in that the reader believes that the story being told is 'the embodiment of something completed. That end, the finished place, is the human being, a body in time and space, telling a story.' In contrast, in the Archive, 'the implicit understanding is that things are not over... not finished... incomplete'.[5] And they will remain so unless we find all the traces and hear all the voices of those who participated in and who felt the impact of the events with which we are concerned. Because of 'all the fragments, traces – all the inchoate stuff – that has ended up in the archive', the possibilities for the story are broader than Daryl's story suggests and than he can possibly know. However, there are still absences, things we cannot find here. The gaps intrigue us and, as Steedman says, we 'read for what is *not* there: the silences and the absences of documents always speak to us'.[6]

For instance, there is an incident in Daryl's story that has reached mythological status in the shared memory of those who participated in the events he describes. This incident is the bulldozing of the bark huts at Jackson's Track, homes in which people had lived for more than twenty years. We know that Daryl witnessed the event. We know that the Neerim Branch of the Aborigines Advancement League 'initiated a move for demolition of the humpies'.[7] We know that all those upon whom it had an impact *heard* that it had happened and talked about it time and again. Yet there is no record that the demolition ever occurred: no letter, no memo, no receipt for services rendered, no account in old Buln Buln Shire Council minutes. Anywhere. The silence is deafening.

Upon first glance, the Archive can seem the antithesis of Memoir. Or, to put this another way, Memoir and the 'written record' are at odds with one another. Or, as Mark Baker says in *The fiftieth gate*, 'the memories and the histories seem to stalk each other'.[8] There are many possible reasons why the demolition is not documented: it was done illegally without the landowner's consent; it was done in secret and so it was covered up; it was considered by the perpetrators to be such a mundane act that no one thought to document it or take responsibility for it. Daryl witnessed the demolition and while it happened he situated himself so he would be seen as a witness when the bulldozers rammed the huts. It seems to me that his presence surrounded the act with guilt. Perhaps, then, the gap in the record is an indication that things have been left out in order to maintain the established story of good citizens doing good things in the name of progress and civilisation.

First council meeting at the Warragul Shire Hall, c1892
Photo by Larry Hills of original photograph held by the Warragul Historical Society

It is one of the purposes of oral history to 'document particular aspects of historical experience which tend to be missing from other sources such as personal relations, domestic work or family life'.[9] But because constructing narratives based on memory is such a subjective exercise, many historians find relying on oral history or Memoir problematic. Often the remembered past, constructed as a narrative for listeners in the present, conflicts with the record because it is essentially an interpretation of what happened. When she describes memory as partial, many-hued and selective, Wendy Lowenstein seems to agree that oral testimony is not pure recovery of the actuality of the past. However, she also declares that '[oral testimony] is far more reliable than the scraps of evidence contained in written records. If you want a date in history go to the records; if you want the flesh and bones, love and hate, ask the people who were alive that day.'[10] It is up to the historian to weigh up one set of information against the other and decide, says Steedman: 'It is the Historian who makes the stuff of the past (Everything) into a structure or an event, a happening or a thing, through the activities of thought and writing.'[11]

When I turn to the Archive looking for clues about the historical events at Jackson's Track, I wonder if Pauline might make an attempt to enter with me, but I do not ask. The National Australian Archive is set up to be accessible, but it is not necessarily easy to enter. These days the researcher is at at an advantage if he or she is computer literate and has some idea of the subject headings and kinds of words archivists use to classify and file documents. The archivist is always willing to help the confused researcher: she works fast, moves from computer to shelves, opens heavy books, scans lists, follows trails until what we are looking for is found. But will we ever be able to find it again? It is like a maze, a labyrinth. Some might call it a game, others a trap. I worry that if Pauline were to enter the archive her curiosity would dissipate the minute she realises that the thousands of pages of old papers, heavy books filled with long lists, the catalogue, the computers filled with written information (a substantial amount of it dedicated solely to interaction with Aboriginal people) were all largely missing the voices of Aboriginals themselves. 'How can so much have been written?' I imagine her saying, 'without anyone asking us?' I am afraid the Archive would show her an abyss between us, just as I am afraid of seeing it myself. Inevitably, when I begin to sift through documents relating to her and her family, I see some of the many, many reasons she would turn away and I understand how terribly she would be let down by the assumptions and value systems of settler Australians. I realise that the Archive is not limitless or all encompassing for her.

The story in the Archive is only one of many stories. It is not the only story. It is my job as the writer to gather all the stories, scour the record, note the silences and ultimately to write my own story, the story Pauline and I need to know in order to finally understand the meaning of what happened all those years ago.

ENDNOTES

1. Warragul Shire no longer exists. It was amalgamated with Buln Buln and Naracan Shires to become Baw Baw Shire in 1992.

2. *The Warragul Gazette*, 'District league has done much to advance welfare for Aborigines', 4 August 1959, p. 19.

3. Carolyn Steedman (2001: 1). Derrida is talking here about the ancient Greek *arkhe* stored in the *arkheion*, where only the *archon*, or magistrate, had access.

4. Steedman (2001, p. 2).

5. Steedman (2001, p. 147).

6. Steedman (2001, pp. 149–151).

7. *The Warragul Gazette*, 'District league has done much to advance welfare for Aborigines', 4 August 1959, p. 19.

8   Mark Baker (1997, p. 52).

9   Perks and Thomson (1998, p. ix).

10   Wendy Lowenstein is quoted in Murphy (1986, p. 162).

11   Steedman (2001, p. 154).

REFERENCES

Baker, Mark. 1997. *The fiftieth gate*. Melbourne: Harper Collins.

Foucault, Michel. 1989. *The archaeology of knowledge*, translated by Smith, Sheridan A. M. London: Routledge.

Murphy, John. 1986. 'The voice of memory: History, autobiography and oral memory'. *Historical studies* 22 (87): 157–175.

Perks, R.; Thomson, A. 1998. 'Introduction'. In *The oral history reader*. London: Routledge.

Steedman, Carolyn. 2001. *Dust*. Manchester: Manchester University Press.

Cite this chapter as: Landon, Carolyn. 2006. 'The story in the archive'. In *Jackson's Track revisited: History, remembrance and reconciliation*. Melbourne: Monash University ePress. pp. 2.1–2.7. DOI: 10.2104/jtr06002.

CHAPTER 3

THE STORY OF THE BOARD

Carolyn Landon

This chapter explores the policy of assimilation through the story of the formation of the Aborigines Welfare Board in 1958. Why was policy change concerning Aboriginal people in Victoria considered necessary at that time? What sort of investigation was carried out to discover the kinds of change needed? Why was assimilation so wholeheartedly embraced as the basis for change? What made policy makers assume that nothing could be more civilised than to welcome Aborigines into White society as equal citizens? Most importantly, why, as Daryl Tonkin remembers, were the people who would be most affected, the Aborigines themselves, deeply angry and afraid? With the benefit of hindsight it is easy to criticise the contents of the McLean Report, the report that led to the Board's formation.

Warragul Shire Hall, now home to the Warragul Historical Society
Photo by Larry Hills of original photograph held by the Warragul Historical Society

Without Pauline, I search articles in the Warragul and Drouin newspapers held at the Warragul Historical Society. However, in my mind she is watching over my shoulder to see what I find. Her spirit reads the reports and the letters with me, her presence forces me to give all the documents I find a personal reading. Through her, I put faces and personalities to the comments made by faceless men. Pauline is a presence behind me asking what proof of truth these archives give, telling me to be careful about what I believe to be true.

Although I am looking for signs of Hector Cowden and find one or two pieces on the activities of the local branch of the Victorian Aborigines Advancement League, the first series of articles I come across show that the new Aborigines Welfare Board was becoming active in the Warragul/Drouin area by 1958, about the time Daryl remembers significant events occurring in his own life at Jackson's Track. Although he was unaware that the old moribund Protection Board had become the Welfare Board, Daryl tells us in his memoir that 'a new policy' was rumoured to be affecting the 'blackfellas':

> The talk continued around the camp fire night after night as stories came through about people actually being put into houses in white neighbourhoods.
>
> 'What do they want to live there for? They don't know anybody?'
>
> ... Once the policy was under way on the missions, they then started rounding up families who lived on crown land along the river banks. The Dimboola families were being shifted. Talk around the camp fire became angry but also fearful.[1]

Articles about the Aborigines Welfare Board send me back to the history books to fill in the gaps in my knowledge. I am aware that the Board was established in 1958 as a result of a one-man Board of Inquiry into the 'Aboriginal problem' in Victoria, and I am aware that the function of the Aborigines Welfare Board was to promote the moral, intellectual and physical welfare of Aborigines with a view to their assimilation into the general community. The writings of the late anthropologist Diane Barwick, and historians Bain Attwood and Heather Goodall fill me in on some of the rest. In her assessment of the success of the Board, Barwick said that its intentions were supposedly benign and that its membership included education, housing and health ministers, as well as five other members, two of whom were required to be Aborigines and one an expert in anthropology or sociology. This combination of members seems reasonable, but Barwick, who was writing about the Board in 1971, stressed that the Board's assimilationist policies proved disastrous.[2] What did she mean? What made them unworkable? Historian Heather Goodall called the Victorian Board policy an 'aggressive' attempt to disperse communities and hinted that the 'Diaspora' was genocidal in that assimilation was an attempt to make the Aborigine disappear.[3]

Of course, in the introduction to her book *Invasion to embassy*, Goodall is commenting on the era of assimilation from a 1990s perspective, from the era of reconciliation. Her book came out just as I had completed a big chunk of Daryl's memoir and was realising that it had the makings of a classic Australian story. In 1996 we had a different point of view from those who were creating policy in 1957. We had a different language. For instance, the word 'invasion', with the particular meaning Goodall gives it, would not have entered the vocabulary of Paul Hasluck, Federal Minister for Territories in the 1950s, or Charles McLean, retired Chief Stipendiary Magistrate who headed a Board of Inquiry into Aboriginal Welfare in Victoria. Although it was a term some Aboriginal activists and certain anthropologists used back then, it had little acceptance; even if it was an acknowledged concept, it carried nowhere near the weight it does today. No, men like Hasluck, good people with honest intentions, but with little insight or direct knowledge of Australian Aboriginal people, believed that assimilation was the only means of 'historical progress'[4] for the 'dark people' (common vernacular back in the 1950s). A. P. Elkin, the most influential anthropologist of the day, who did have direct knowledge of Aboriginal people, also argued for a policy that would 'assist the Aborigines to make their own way in the [White Australian] community as full citizens'.[5] Perhaps if they had understood our modern concept of 'invasion' and all it implies about the Aboriginal point of view and who we settler Australians are in relation to Aboriginal Australians, they might have recognised the incompatibility between their assumptions and their good intentions.

Once I have absorbed this information, I turn back to the old newsprint and come across an article in the *Warragul Gazette* dated 18 March 1958. It reports that at the second Aboriginal State Conference in Newmerella (run by, according to the *Gazette*, the Australian Aboriginal Council, but more likely by the Council for Aboriginal Rights), as many as one-hundred 'natives' from all parts of Victoria discussed the appointment of Harold Blair and Pastor Doug Nicholls to the newly formed Aborigines Welfare Board.[6] Pauline has told me that her Pop, as she called her grandfather, Stewart Hood, and Eugene Mobourne, a good mate of her dad's at the Track, were active in Aboriginal campaigns back then and so I imagine those two elders from the Track might have been at that meeting. I wonder what kind of debate took place over the appointment of these two Aboriginal men. Both men had high profiles amongst White Australians; Nicholls for his sporting achievements and mission work, and Blair for his fine tenor voice. In

Victims or victors, a historical account of the Victorian Aborigines Advancement League, Geraldine Briggs implies their appointment was a publicity stunt.[7] I wonder if the people who read this article in their local weekly paper in 1958 had any idea these might not be universally approved appointments. Or if they even cared.

I come across an article in the *Warragul Gazette* from 22 July 1958 that interests me. It is a report of a talk given by the anthropologist Dr Donald Thomson who has 'deeply stirred the Warragul audience' with accounts of 'how bitterly ashamed' he is about 'our treatment of aborigines'. The article also notes that the 'Professor of Anthropology at Melbourne University' was a 'recent appointee' to the new Aborigines Welfare Board.[8] I have read some of Thomson's work on Aborigines and realise his importance in Aboriginal policy-making throughout Australia. His influence was as great as the legendary A. P. Elkin, with whom he competed and sometimes squabbled.[9] I am surprised to find him addressing a meeting in Warragul – until I see that his brother-in-law, Mr Wally McColl, is a local man.

Thomson was an interesting man: a man ahead of, yet also of, his time. He, more than any other anthropologist, according to Bain Attwood, knew Aboriginal cultures and had come to love, in particular, the Yolngu people in Arnhem Land with whom he lived for several years in the 1930s. His field work there informed his thinking for most of his life. Only Thomson seemed to understand the concept of Aboriginal sovereignty and he understood that their deep connection with the land gave Yolngu people the right to defend themselves against White man's aggression. Only he seemed to realise that the concept of assimilation meant the death of 'culture', a disaster he believed had already occurred in Victoria. Thomson believed that Aboriginal Australians had the 'right' to a life 'independent of white men's law and culture'.[10] Here was a man who, as he wrote in response to a request for help from Bill Onus (president of the Australian Aborigines League), 'wished that I myself were an Aborigine so that I had the right to fight with you'.[11] He also realised that 'every white man approaches the subject of the administration of the aborigines with a superiority complex – the assumption that the native culture is inferior and must be changed or eliminated'.[12]

When I read these things about Donald Thomson, it seems to me that while he lived in the era of assimilation, he belonged in the era of reconciliation. As it turns out, he could not escape his context when it came to the question of Aboriginal people of mixed blood, or 'half-castes', as they were known. These Aboriginals made up most of the Aboriginal population in south-east Australia. Thomson, along with Elkin, argued that the detribalised, mixed-race people of Aboriginal descent found in Victoria had largely lost their culture; that 'changed circumstances and altered environments' meant they had lost their Aboriginal identity as well.[13] 'With the people of mixed blood,' he wrote in 1945, 'there can only be one policy – that of advance and education. They are not aborigines and cannot be treated as such. They must be treated as white men'.[14]

I shake my head when I think of Thomson on the Board. How, I wonder, could a man who believed there was no Aboriginal culture or identity in Victoria sit on a Board that was supposed to promote Aboriginal welfare? It was only later, after he had met and spent time with the people fighting for Lake Tyers,[15] that Thomson realised how wrong he was about culture and Aboriginal identity in the south. In 1963, after his time at Lake Tyers, Thomson wrote a letter to *The Age* stating, 'The policy of "assimilation" which is being implemented in this State and elsewhere in the Commonwealth appears to be directed at the breaking down of the communal and family life of the Aborigines, and in Victoria, of dispersing them over the State... I believe that our paramount concern must be for the welfare of these people and that their dispersal throughout the State is not consistent with this objective.'[16] But that was too late for this story.

I wonder, peering at flaking pages of old newspapers in the dimly lit rooms of the Historical Society, what Pauline would think of Thomson and the Board. I wonder if she has ever heard of them, and if so, how much she knows. For instance, why was policy change concerning Aboriginal people in Victoria considered necessary in the mid-1950s? What indications were there to warrant change? What sort of investigation was carried out to discover the kinds of change needed? Who did the investigating? Why was assimilation so wholeheartedly embraced as the basis for change? What kinds of practical measures were recommended and adopted to effect change? Most importantly, why, as Daryl remembers, were the people who would be most affected, the Aborigines themselves, deeply angry and afraid? The articles in the local papers go some way to answering those questions, but they are only the beginning.

I turn to the National Archives in the Public Records Office of Victoria where, as I have discovered searching the Internet, there are documents relating to the establishment, in 1958, of the Aborigines' Welfare Board. I find Charles McLean's *Report Upon the Operation of the Aborigines Act 1928* to the Victorian Parliament, tabled 18 January 1957. Each new document I find forces me to ask new questions. I turn once more to the history books to discover why the inquiry was conducted and then tabled at that time. It turns out that although the report was tabled not long after Henry Bolte took over the reins of power in Victoria, it came out of a Board of Inquiry that the embattled Labour Premier, John Cain, had been forced to appoint in 1953 as a concession to pressure from the vocal middle class who were freshly concerned about the 'Aboriginal problem' in the state.[17] I need to go back even further into the past to discover the historical reasons for this new awareness of the Aboriginal presence in the state.

The historians tell us that just before the Second World War, in 1939, the Aboriginal people walked off Cumeragunja Station in New South Wales in protest over living conditions, human rights and natural justice. In spite of general indifference to the event among the White community, it was a major event that had a profound effect on the thinking of Aboriginal people involved.[18] However, as a result of the walk-off, or 'strike' as it was called at the time, there was a movement of Aboriginal people into Victoria, where groups of people formed camps on the flats along the Murray River near Barmah and at the 'Daisy Patch' (a common name for a camp at Daish's Paddock) on the Goulbourn River near Mooroopna. With the onset of the War, there was a general movement of Aboriginal people across the state as work patterns shifted to accommodate the war effort and Aboriginal men joined up. Control of Aboriginal movement from the missions such as Cumeragunia and Lake Tyers eased during the War, and as a result camps and fringe communities sprang up in many places. Jackson's Track was one of these places. Also, a large congregation of women and children, and some men, gathered in Fitzroy in Melbourne to await the return of relatives who were soldiers. After the War, when people's minds were back on local issues, the presence of Aboriginal people living in humpies on the rivers at the fringes of towns seemed to alarm and concern the general public.

There was also a new breed of Aboriginal man about – the returned soldier. Daryl tells in his memoir of a fellow named Jack Patten who came to work at the Track in the late 1940s.

> Some like Bob Nelson and Jack Patten, had been soldiers in the Australian Army and had been restless and on the move ever since the end of the war... They had seen the world and had learned about the possibilities in life... but all doors were shut to them in the towns and so they resigned themselves to pick up an axe... There was a lingering resentment in their bearing... and it was hard to know if they would settle here.[19]

Patten is an interesting case for he was a well-known rights activist in New South Wales before the War, a campaigner and instigator of the Cumeragunja Strike. After the War, he and many others like him, men who had dedicated their lives to the social good of their people and who had served their country in time of war, now found themselves side-lined and looking for work. Daryl tells us a story about Patten that is told time and again all over Australia. Patten went into the pubs in Drouin thinking he would be able to drink with the other men there, but the police in town – in this case one particular policeman known as Up-the-Lane Jack to the families living on the Track – thought this behaviour too cocky and so he was beaten up regularly and sent on his way. Dispirited and frustrated he was a man ripe for angry agitation with nowhere to go. Men like him were alarming to the settled and civilised White public.

In the late 1940s and continuing on into the 1950s the plight of Aboriginal people in Australia came to the attention of the international community. This happened due to protests over a rocket range in central Australia, protests mounted by Aboriginal and non-Aboriginal protesters alike to protect the tribal people who lived in the path of rockets. Calls for human rights and natural justice for Aboriginal people were countered by claims of Communist incitement, and soon the protest was defeated by the usual political and bureaucratic indifference. However, this issue came together with the un-usually high visibility of Aboriginal people in the city (and on the fringes of towns and on the roads) to plant a seed of consciousness, or perhaps guilt, in the mind of the gen-eral public.

Politicians, social workers and clergy alike began to refer to the 'Aboriginal problem'[20] in Victoria. Groups such as Women's International League for Peace and Freedom, Apex, and the Victorian Aboriginal Group (all of whose members were largely White, middle class and Christian) put pressure on the Victorian government. They called for the public to develop a conscience concerning the condition of Victorian Aborigines and they wanted to know why Victoria was lagging behind the rest of the country.[21] The high visibility of a 'largely itinerant population of Aborigines without strong family ties in Melbourne who came to the city looking for work and found themselves homeless, hopeless and without clearly defined avenues of assistance'[22] fed right into assimilationist theories that were re-gaining momentum[23] around the country. In 1955 Henry Bolte, the then Victorian Premier, finally gave in to pressure and re-appointed Charles McLean to form a one-man Board of Inquiry. Bolte made certain that the terms of reference ensured that McLean would 'broaden Victoria's definition of Aboriginality to include large numbers of mixed descent Aboriginal people, and that he [would] formulate methods by which Aboriginal people could be assimilated into the Anglo-Australian society'.[24] In other words, as Heather Goodall would argue, he wanted McLean to find a way to make the problem disappear.

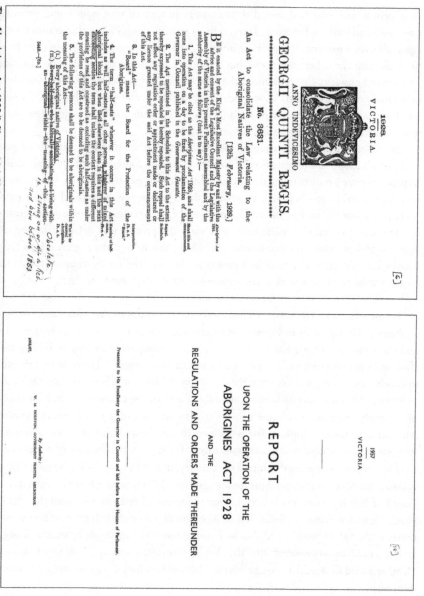

The *Aborigines Act 1928* (left) on which McLean's report (right) was based
(Hand-written notes are from the original document)
National Archives of Australia: B408, 10

Did anyone have a real sense of the impact that the idea of assimilation would have on the lives of Aboriginal people in general and the Jackson's Track people in particular? It seems to me, reading historical accounts and looking back on these old documents from my vantage point in the late twentieth century, that assimilation as it was being promoted by Paul Hasluck, Federal Minister for Territories in the 1950s,[25] was doomed because of its failure to consult Aboriginal people themselves. As Hasluck confirmed in 1951, the official objective of assimilation 'means, in practical terms, that, in the course of time, it is expected that all persons of Aboriginal blood or mixed blood in Australia will live like White Australians do'.[26] His meaning here seems to be that Aboriginal people would have the same opportunities, education and civil rights as all other Australians. He was talking about the idea of 'One People'.[27] Hasluck said, 'There can be no doubt that *the only* possible future for the very small minority of Aboriginal people in Australia today is to merge into and be received as full members of the great community of... European persons which surrounds them.'[28] It must have seemed a generous policy offered to what was then considered a benighted people by an enlightened and civilised society. Hasluck went on to say this would 'require many years of slow, patient endeavour'.[29] Although he did not elaborate on his meaning in that respect, it is clear he assumed that all Aboriginal people would, if they were not already, be willing to forego their heritage and adopt the obviously superior living standards and cultural practices of Anglo-Australian society.[30] It was assumed by bureaucrats and policy makers that all right thinking, humanitarian and Christian people in the non-Aboriginal world would unanimously endorse Hasluck's view as the best way to solve the 'Aboriginal problem'. What could be more civilised than to welcome Aborigines into White society as equal citizens? It was a gift to the 'dark people'.

In fact, when McLean finally tabled his report, White campaigners criticised it. They pointed out that Aboriginal rights activists had been arguing for citizenship, civil and economic rights for most of the century but that they wanted integration not assimilation. Anna Vroland, a writer and radio commentator as well as honorary secretary of Women's Internatinal League for Peace and Freedom, had had close contact with the women at Lake Tyers. She realised something other White campaigners had missed: that 'social acceptance by their own people still meant more to most Aborigines than did assimilation into the general community'.[31] Vroland had been campaigning against assimilation since the 1930s and was one of only a handful of White Australians to publicly oppose the policy. She insisted that Aboriginal people should have the 'freedom to identify themselves as a people' and she confronted anthropologists such as Elkin and Thomson, as well as politicians. Unfortunately, no one was listening. Criticism by Vroland was drowned out by the great acclaim that met the report when it was tabled. It seemed that officially there was no recognition that many of the south-eastern Aboriginal people would resist McLean's version of assimilation, and no understanding that many would reject better material living conditions in favour of maintaining their culture. It seemed that only one campaigner in all of Victoria, Vroland, considered that they had any culture still intact. A mere 24 hours after the McLean report was presented, the Victorian Parliament announced that the recommendations in the report would become law.[32]

I read the McLean report in the large reading room at the Public Records Office in North Melbourne. The report is dated 1957 and is written on thin, yellowing foolscap paper. It is 22 pages of single-spaced 10-point Times New Roman font and is accompanied by an annotated and underlined 1928 Aborigines Act. The report is addressed to 'His Excellency General Sir Reginald Dallas Brooks, Knight Commander of the Most Honourable order of Bath...' etc. The language of the report begins in a formal tone, but quickly becomes a personal narrative of MacLean's visits to mission stations and country towns, his conversations with this fellow or that, people he thought seemed to know something about Aborigines. From these experiences he draws conclusions. With the benefit of hindsight and with the absent Pauline's spirit looking over my shoulder and metaphorically digging me in the back to make me pay attention, I find it easy to criticise the contents of the report.

In the course of his investigation McLean spoke with many people connected with the 'Aboriginal problem' including the manager of Lake Tyers, Mr L. Rule, and his predecessor, Major Glen, as well as officers of the Housing Commission, Education Department, Commonwealth Employment Department and Health Department. In all this discussion, it seems he spoke with only two Aboriginal leaders, Pastor Doug Nicholls and Shadrach James, both from Cumeragunja in New South Wales. It seems he spoke to no Victorian Aborigines, and there is no reference in the entire report to any of the advice McLean may have received from Nicholls and James.

One of McLean's terms of reference was to discover the number, distribution and living conditions of Aboriginal people living in Victoria. He asked help from police to locate and count – and sometimes name – the Aboriginal people in each district. He concluded:

> To complete the specific information required under this heading, the returns furnished to me by the police show that of a total of 287 who

are capable of working, 177 are classified as 'regularly employed'. In addition, 45 residents of Lake Tyers are capable of working, and are given some employment at the station. The distribution of the largest groups, apart from those I have specifically mentioned [the camps at Mooroopna and Barmah] is as follows: -- Nathalia, 150; Orbost (including Newmerella and Waygara), 150; Robinvale, 75; Dimboola and Antwerp, 65; Heywood, 55; and Echuca, 53.[33]

This can't be right, I think. He hasn't mentioned the camp at Jackson's Track, a large, functioning community of, according to Daryl, about 150 people. Why hadn't he known about Jackson's Track? How many other people had he missed? In a box brought to me by the Public Records Office archivist, I locate a folder labelled 'McLean Inquiry: Police Reports and Population Details'. In this folder is a letter to Mr McLean from Mr Richards, Superintendent of Police in Warragul, dated 23 April 1956.[34] In this letter, written in awkward longhand, Richards states 'Inquiries throughout this district have failed to locate any aboriginal natives residing therein'.[35] Later, on the 30 May 1956, the Superintendent sent an official report: 'Most of the Aboriginals seen about these parts are connected with the settlement at Lake Tyres [sic] and only visit here on seasonal work.'[36] Here is a gap, just as Carolyn Steedman said there would be,[37] a silence that speaks loudly. I can feel Pauline's wonder. Is she shocked and angry that her people were passed over? Or is she laughing at their luck? I try to work it out. Was the assertion that there were no Aboriginal people in the area a political statement or a ruse to cover the practices of the Drouin police in their dealings with the Jackson's Track mob? Daryl tells us that they had established a curfew that applied only to the Aboriginal people; that they had the habit of beating offenders and sending them on their way; that Jackson's Track was always the first port of call for the police if anything untoward was happening in the Drouin area. Perhaps the superintendent thought the police had the 'blackfellas' well in hand and wanted no interference from any Board. Thus, the silence about the existence of Aborigines in their midst. Perhaps, on the other hand, he was truly ignorant of their presence. Much later, when I ask locals about this omission their response is 'Those Aboriginal people would have been well-known to the police, at least, some of them would have been'.[38] But as became obvious when Daryl's book came out, many people in the local area were actually as unaware of the Aboriginal presence at the Track as Richards seemed to be then. Out of sight out of mind, I think. Certainly McLean was kept in the dark.

Courtesy of Museum Victoria: Registration No. XP 1565. Photographer: Richard Seeger

The family at Jackson's Track
Reproduced with permission also from Regina Rose

If it is so easy to see one such gaping hole in McLean's report, then how many others will there be? I wonder how McLean could make decisions that would affect people's lives when he didn't know who the people were and had never spoken with them? One of the most important aspects of McLean's report was that he had to determine who was actually an Aborigine – that is a person 'of not less that one-fourth part aboriginal blood' as defined by the state.[39] In his report, he said it was difficult to assess the percentage of blood in many cases because 'over the succeeding generations, dating from the very early days of settlement until now, there had been such a high degree of miscegenation and sexual promiscuity on the part of aboriginal women and white men'.[40] I can hear Pauline ask 'What's this *miscegenation?* Sounds like a disease. What is it?' And, in fact, that is exactly what she says when, weeks later, I show her the report and ask her what she thinks. Both she and I see the negativity in the word and the thoughts behind the word, but I wonder if she knows the history of McLean's thinking?

The 'half-caste problem' had been plaguing the state since the 1860s when the reality of 'interbreeding' became obvious. Back then the concept of 'racial miscegenation' assumed that 'hybrids' showed increasing signs of degeneration and that 'in Australia, the children of black women by white fathers are worse than the pure blacks in many particulars'. Thus, 'the Aboriginal-European population... posed a national problem' and throughout Australia 'officialdom had the power to prevent sexual contacts between white and black, and commonly discouraged the rare European who wished to establish a legal relationship with an Aborigine'.[41]

This thinking, left over from the nineteenth century but obviously still current in 1957, relates directly to Pauline's parents, to the act of mixing-blood as Daryl and Euphie did with their nine children. The word 'miscegenation', coupled with the term 'sexual promiscuity', is a terrible judgement on Pauline's parents and on Pauline herself: it declares that her mother was 'loose', and that Pauline is tainted with a kind of disease. However, by the 1950s the emphasis on genetics was changing to that of culture. When McLean emphasised the white blood running in the veins of the half-caste he was attempting to find a way to bring the degenerate and clearly doomed Aborigine into the White Australian way of life. By emphasising the white blood in Pauline's veins, the concept negates her Aboriginal identity, which is paramount to her.

The words 'miscegenation' and 'sexual promiscuity' may also be seen from a modern context as a judgement on women in Pauline's family who had left untenable relationships and, in practical ways, sought security for themselves and their children with other men. It is useful to remember that in the 1950s in the non-Aboriginal world, domestic violence was never spoken about, divorce was rare, unwed mothers were shunned, and deviations from the norm of the 'respectable' nuclear family were covered up as far as possible. In the eyes of the middle class Christians who controlled social mores, Aboriginal women who openly defied the norm degraded those mores. Charles McLean, long time public servant, 'conscientious, noble and merciful' magistrate for thirty-four years,[42] couldn't help himself when he chose the words 'miscegenation' and 'sexual promiscuity' to put in his report. Women who left their husbands, who had children with other men, were degraded – especially when they were Aborigines, a people supposedly with no culture and no identity.

McLean, a retired magistrate, could not easily shake off his belief in genetics, even though his task was to effect social/cultural change and bring the Aboriginal people in from the cold, so to speak. For instance, in a discussion of 'the capacity of people of aboriginal blood to live and maintain themselves and their families according to the general standards of the Victorian community', [43] he focused on the mental capacity of Aboriginal people:

> Most authorities now agree that there is no innate racial inferiority of intelligence in the aborigine. In any case, there is a preponderance of white blood among those in Victoria, though some degree of degeneration from the general average of the white race might perhaps be expected from the fact that much of the white parentage has had its origin in the association of 'sub-standard' whites.[44]

This makes me cringe for upon reading these remarks I am taken back to my own childhood when I marvelled at the stories my grandfather told me about the American Indians and took as truth his pronouncement that those Whites who mingled with Cherokee 'squaws' were degenerate. Now, fifty years later, I recoil at my young self, and at McLean whose opinions held the weight of authority. Although he had never met Daryl Tonkin, a man I hold in high esteem and know to be generous and honest, it feels to me as if McLean were talking specifically about him and calling him degenerate merely by fact of his association with Aborigines. At the same time as he declared the racial equality of Aboriginals, McLean belittled people of mixed racial parentage like Pauline, people whose intelligence he admitted was in evidence but who he nonetheless assumed to be faulty since their fathers were seen to be sub-standard. For the most part, this giving with one hand and taking with the other seems to have been an unconscious act. Yet how obvious it is to me now looking back. It seems to me that McLean could not see his condescension any more than my grandfather could. I know now, with the aid of hindsight, that the constructions McLean, as a settler Australian, used to understand Aboriginal people were at odds with how the people themselves constructed their identities, and at that point in our history McLean seemed to have no means of altering these preconceptions.

At one point in the report it is clear that McLean was indeed not conscious of his assumptions. One of his tasks was to discover if there might be any impediment or obstacle that lay in the path of 'economic absorption', as he called one aspect of assimil-ation. He identified 'faults' in the Aboriginal character such as living for the present with 'lack of thought for tomorrow', strong family ties, the 'habit' of sharing 'which is deeply rooted among them', the 'unhopeful' atmosphere of their homes, 'lack of initiative', and sense of 'inferiority due to environment'. These were all his words and the tone was one of pathos mixed with disgust and incomprehension, but the pity and condescension is a construction of the times. He almost redeemed himself by admitting that another obstacle to economic absorption might be the attitude of White people, which he said could be patronising and superior. But he went on to say that in the face of White superiority, 'the shy reserve of the dark people develops into somewhat resentful and suspicious outlook towards any friendly approach by the whites'.[45] From this it is clear who he thought was at fault, and even though he actually used the word 'superiority', he did not seem to have any idea of his own sense of superiority and was therefore unaware that this attitude of racial superiority would undermine the policy he was creating.

Everything McLean wrote in the report supported the idea of assimilation. He con-cluded that assimilation would solve all ills, yet he did not recommend the sale of Lake Tyers. It seems that his own prejudices about Aboriginal people allowed him to assume that the inherent faults he could not help naming in his report would render them intract-able. He recommended the formation of a Welfare Board with membership including three Aboriginal people. The Parliament appointed only two, as we have seen: Pastor Doug Nicholls and Harold Blair.

Daryl Tonkin understood, sitting by the fire all those years ago talking to his Abori-ginal family and friends, that they were angry and afraid, but he had no idea how public thought was changing and how it was about to affect his world. Even as he told his story almost 40 years after the events, he was still unaware how theories of anthropologists, rights advocates and public policy makers worked. For instance, Daryl has no idea even now that his dated and unconscious use of the word 'full-blood' in describing Stewart Hood has a historical context: historically, policy making around Aborigines has been dependent upon theoretical racial categories such as 'full-blood' and 'half-caste'. Daryl has no idea that his family was eventually torn asunder because it was assumed that the Aboriginal people on his land were all half-castes and therefore their Aboriginality was erased. He doesn't know that the word 'Aborigine' is itself a colonial word that in the Australian settler society has served to homogenise a diverse people into one racial group that can be easily defined as 'Other' and therefore served by simplistic and racially de-termined public policy. This definition of people by their 'breed' was used to break up Coranderrk in the 1880s, to justify assimilation in mid-twentieth century Victoria and is used now to undermine native title claims. But all Daryl knows about it is that he has somehow been betrayed by History, which somehow destroyed what he valued in life.

ENDNOTES

1. Landon and Tonkin (1999, p. 248).

2. Barwick (1971, p. 173).

3. Goodall (1996, p. 310).

4. Attwood (2003, p. xii).

5. Attwood (2003, p. 116).

6. *Warragul Gazette*, 'Welfare of Aborigines', 18 March 1958, p. 12.

7. Anonymous (1985, p. 49).

8. *Warragul Gazette*, 'Ashamed of our treatment of aborigines', 22 July 1958, p. 18.

9. Attwood (2003, pp. 102–112).

10. Attwood (2003, p. 116).

11. Attwood (2003, p. 103).

12. Attwood (2003, p. 118).

13. Kerin (1999, p. 3).

14. Kerin (1999, p. 124).

15. From the moment the Aborigines Welfare Board was formed in 1958 there began a thirteen-year struggle to retain Lake Tyers for its residents. In July 1971 the government passed the Aboriginal Lands Act, which 'made the 4000 acres comprising theLake Tyers reserve the freehold property of an Aboriginal Trust made up of Lake Tyers residents' (Anonymous 1985, p. 81).

16. Donald Thomson, letter to *The Age*, 23 May 1963.

17. Anonymous 1985, pp. 46–47.

18. Anonymous 1985, p. 39.

19. Landon and Tonkin (1999, p. 171).

20. McLean, Charles, *Report upon the Operation of the Aborigines Act 1928 and the Regulations and Order made Thereunder*, Melbourne 1957, B408, McLean Inquiry, Item 10, p. 8.

21. Corinne Manning (2002, p. 173).

22. Anonymous (1985, p. 41).

23. Assimilation, as an idea, had been determining policy since the 1880's when Victoria, in an attempt to save money, tried to create a climate of assimilation for 'half-caste' Aborigines who were banned from the mission stations. Racial prejudice seemed to defeat this social

experiment and left many half-castes destitute so they were re-admitted onto the missions at the turn of the century although the determination of Aboriginality by 'blood' was not changed. It wasn't until McLean made his report in 1956 that Victoria recognised the Aboriginality of 'half-caste' people. See Manning (2002, p. 159); Attwood (2003, p. 118). Yet still, in 1968, when I arrived in Victoria people were discounting the presence of Aboriginal people in Victoria by saying there were no full-bloods here.

24   Manning (2002, p. 159).

25   Assimilation was adopted as a policy by the Federal Government in the 1937 Native Welfare Conference. However its implementation was delayed by the outbreak of WWII and was not revived until Paul Hasluck was appointed the Federal Minister for Territories in May 1951. In September 1951, Hasluck urged government delegates at the Australian Native Welfare Conference to revitalise the 1937 decision and implement assimilation-style Aboriginal welfare policies. Victoria was the last state to do so Manning (2002, p. 160).

26   'Native Welfare in Australia', page 3, An address given by the Minister For Territories The Honourable Paul Hasluck M.P., to the Baptist Home Mission Rally, Sydney, 14 February 1956.

27   Paul Hasluck 'Native Welfare in Australia', p. 3.

28   Paul Hasluck 'Native Welfare in Australia', p. 3.

29   Macintyre (1999, p. 220).

30   Manning (2002, p. 160).

31   Kerin (1999, p. 26).

32   *The Age*, 'Report on Board of Inquiry,' 1 February 1957.

33   B408, McLean Inquiry, Item 10, *McLean Report*, p. 21. McLean, Charles, *Report upon the Operation of the Aborigines Act 1928 and the Regulations and Order made Thereunder*, Melbourne 1957, p. 8.

34   B408/0 *McLean Inquiry: Police Reports & Population Details*, letter 23 April 1956.

35   B408/0 *McLean Inquiry*.

36   B408/0 *McLean Inquiry*, report 30 May, 1956.

37   Steedman (2001, pp. 149–151).

38   Interview with Mr Alwyn Jensen, Neerim South, 8 April 2004.

39   B408, McLean Inquiry, Item 10, *McLean Report*, p. 6.

40   B408, McLean Inquiry, Item 10, *McLean Report*, p. 6.

41   Beckett (1988, 197–199).

[42]   Manning (2002, p. 163).

[43]   B408, McLean Inquiry, Item 10, *McLean Report*, p. 8.

[44]   B408, McLean Inquiry, Item 10, *McLean Report*, p. 8.

[45]   B408, McLean Inquiry, Item 10, *McLean Report*, p 10.

REFERENCES

Anonymous. 1985. *Victims or victors? The story of the Victorian Aborigines Advancement League.* Melbourne: Hyland House Publishing.

Attwood, Bain. 2003. *Rights for Aborigines.* Sydney: Allen & Unwin.

Barwick, Diane. 1971. '20 changes in the Aboriginal population of Victoria, 1863–1966'. In *Aboriginal man and environment in Australia,* edited by Mulvaney, J.; Goss, J. Canberra: Australian National University Press.

Beckett, Jeremy. 1988. *The past in the present; The present in the past: Constructing a national Aboriginality.* Canberra: Aboriginal Studies Press for the Australian Institute of Aboriginal Studies.

Goodall, Heather. 1996. *Invasion to embassy: Land in Aboriginal politics in New South Wales, 1770–1972.* Sydney, Australia: Allen & Unwin.

Kerin, Sitarani. 1999. *An attitude of respect: Anna Vroland and Aboriginal rights, 1947–1957.* Melbourne: Monash Publications in History.

Landon, Carolyn; Tonkin, Daryl. 1999. *Jackson's Track: Memoir of a Dreamtime place.* Melbourne: Penguin.

Macintyre, Stuart. 1999. *A concise history of Australia.* Melbourne: Cambridge University Press.

Manning, Corinne 2002. 'The McLean report: Legitimising Victoria's new assimilationism'. *Aboriginal history* 26: 159–176.

Steedman, Carolyn. 2001. *Dust.* Manchester: Manchester University Press.

Cite this chapter as: Landon, Carolyn. 2006. 'The story of the Board'. In *Jackson's Track revisited: History, remembrance and reconciliation.* Melbourne: Monash University ePress. pp. 3.1–3.18. DOI: 10.2104/jtr06003.

CHAPTER 4

⭘ THE STORY OF THE LEAGUE

Carolyn Landon

In this chapter, which explores the Victorian Aborigines Advancement League, the facts in the record begin to diverge from Daryl Tonkin's memory. What are the implications of the differences that emerge from his memoir? What does this say about memory versus the record? Is there really a conflict or does one complement the other? What was the League and why is it that evangelistic Christians made up most of the membership of the local branch? The historian finds, by exploring both memory and the record, that the fabric of story deepens and the idea of truth becomes complex and fluid. Point of view, context, narrative structures, subtexts, telling the past for the present, experience and remembrance, attitudes and assumptions all come into play.

I now know something about the Aborigines Welfare Board, its policies and underlying prejudices, but I still do not know how it became active in the local area when the existence of an Aboriginal presence here seemed to be officially unrecognised. There is very little about Board activities, after those initial reports on the members, in the local papers. There is, on the other hand, a great deal about the activities of the Neerim Branch of the Victorian Aborigines Advancement League. What was the League? How did it come into existence? What did it stand for? And why is it that mostly evangelistic Christians made up the membership in the local branch?

Three weeks after Charles Mclean tabled his report, the Victorian Aborigines Advancement League was formed. It arose out of a public meeting called by the Save the Aborigines Committee on 5 February, 1957.[1] The Committee had been formed expressly to come to the aid of the Warburton Ranges Aborigines, who were victims of the joint British-Australian rocket range project begun ten years earlier, and who were now living in appalling conditions. The Committee called the public meeting in direct response to films a Ministerial Study Group had made about their visit to the Warburton Ranges. Doug Nicholls had been a member of the study group and was now showing the public films of diseased, malnourished, and desperate Aboriginal people who had been neglected and left destitute. At the meeting were 'energetic, influential and dedicated people', Doris Blackburn, Gordon Bryant, Stan Davey and Doug Nicholls among them.[2] These experienced campaigners must have discussed the implications of McLean's report[3] at the Save the Aborigines meeting. According to the official history of the Victorian Aborigines Advancement League – *Victims or victors?*, published in 1985 – they agreed then that the threat of the McLean Report's assimilation policies becoming law heightened the need for a broad-based umbrella organisation that could deal with Aboriginal needs on many fronts. In due time the League was created, with far-reaching objectives that reflected past campaigns for Aboriginal rights and also confronted present threats. Their objectives were:

> ...to achieve citizenship rights for Aborigines throughout the Common-
> wealth, to work towards the integration of Aboriginal people with the
> rest of the community while fully recognising the unique contribution
> they were able to make, to attempt to co-ordinate the different Abori-
> ginal welfare organisations operating in Victoria, and to establish a
> general policy of advancement for Aboriginal people.[4]

Other objectives were: equal pay for equal work, free and compulsory education for 'detribalised' Aborigines, and absolute retention of all remaining reserves under Aboriginal communal ownership. The League worked quietly at first, establishing a hostel for Aboriginal girls who came to the city to work. But it came to national attention when it launched a campaign to establish a defence fund for Aborigines that was used to fight for Albert Namatjira, the painter who was arrested and thrown in jail for supplying alcohol to his kin. Widespread support for the League grew and branches began to spring up everywhere.

It was about this time that the League started up in the Drouin/ Neerim South area. Mr B. T. (Bert) Clarke was the school master or head teacher at Neerim East Primary School, which is now situated on good roads fifteen minutes drive north of Warragul and fifteen minutes drive west of Jackson's Track. Back then, on unmade roads, the distances must have seemed daunting. He was also a lay preacher in the Methodist Church and a concerned citizen whose interest focused particularly on the plight of Aboriginal people. He must have known about the camp at the Track, and he must have known Pastor Doug held monthly services there if the weather was fine. I cannot work out whether he knew Nicholls first because of his connection with the Church, and through him found out about the existence of the large camp of Aboriginal people, or whether it was the other way around. Whichever, those who remember Bert Clarke reckon he had a life-long passion for Aboriginal issues and that he was a very good preacher.

It was Clarke who arranged for Pastor Doug to come to the RSL Hall in Warragul to show the Warburton Ranges film and 'speak of the plight of the Australian aborigines', as it was reported in *The Warragul Gazette* on 10 October 1957. Nicholls also screened another film about Albert Namatjira, whom he called 'a great Australian and typical of a great race'. He went on to say, according to the précis of his speech in the article, that:

> Australian natives were not a primitive people but a people living in primitive conditions. They were the aristocrats who were entitled to a better deal than they were receiving from the white people.
>
> ... The aborigines over the centuries had solved their economic and social problems, while those problems for the white race contained the germs for people's destruction.
>
> The white race could not force its so-called civilisation on the aborigines who had no desire to be assimilated. They were a virile race pauperised by the dole system. If given the opportunity they could 'fly high' but they had been denied their rights by being kept a race apart.[5]

As I look at this article I am acutely aware how my friendship with Pauline keeps intruding into my reading; her point of view makes me change my position, my social and psychological context, if you will, and deconstruct the language. I know she doesn't see herself as a race of people, as an Aborigine, the way Nicholls is describing her. She sees herself as the member of a family, a Kurnai woman, more particularly a Brabralung woman, who lives on particular country. In his attempt to get the non-Aboriginal people in his audience to pay attention to him, Pastor Doug uses colonial metaphors and homogenises the people he is speaking about into one type of person, one caste. Pauline would say Namatjira is typical of no one but himself, and owes loyalty only to his family and his country. Nicholls talks here in terms of race: *great race, white race, virile race, race apart*. Nicholls himself is playing the role of race representative, and he is pushing a line of race pride that the Aboriginal rights activists of the time adhered to. But from my modern viewpoint I can see he is undermining himself and his cause in the eyes of Pauline. No wonder Nicholls was mistrusted – as I find out later – amongst the Aboriginal people at the Track and no wonder a certain kind of people responded to his call.

Not long before this large meeting in the RSL Hall, Bert Clarke had asked Doug Nicholls to preach at the Methodist Church in Neerim South. After his sermon Clarke called for formation of the Neerim Branch of the League, and a small group of people must have come together to form an executive. After the large meeting at the RSL Hall, there was a surge of membership and for a while the Neerim Branch had as many as fifty members who were active in town and on the Track, but numbers soon reduced to a core group of workers. As I read more and more articles in the local papers about League activities, the names begin to condense and certain people begin to stand out. They are the names on the list Janet Cowden first showed me in her father's papers; they are the names I first became acquainted with in Daryl's memoir as the do-gooders; they all identify first as Christians, second as citizens. They are: Mr Alwyn Jensen, Mr and Mrs W. H. Buchanan, Mr Hector Cowden, and Mr and Mrs Schouller.

Pastor Doug Nicholls, and Roy Rose with guitar
Photo courtesy of the Mullett family

The local newspapers in the Historical Society are sprinkled with articles about League activities: they held a singalong one Wednesday afternoon in 1958 where 'little aborigine children sang religious choruses to members of the Warragul Branch of the Women's Christian Temperance Union in the Methodist Hall'; they more than once showed the tragic Warburton Ranges film to different groups, thus promoting the idea that Aborigines were a group of wretched people, engendering guilt amongst middle class whites and appealing to the missionary zeal of others; they disseminated educational material to various bodies in the district; they arranged for Donald Thomson to speak about his expedition to find the remote desert Bindibu Tribe, a journey 'six thousand miles [*sic*] from Alice Springs'. For an audience of young farmers, Rotary, and Apex members, Thomson compared the 'happy, carefree and robust' tribal people with those wretched westernised Victorian Aborigines who, in his opinion at that time, had lost their culture and could no longer be called tribal. He entreated the audience to 'share with me the feeling that they are our responsibility and that we must help them to adapt themselves to the changed way of life we have imposed on them'.[6]

Here the League seems to be condoning, through their guest speaker, patriarchal and assimilationist attitudes. This must have been done unconsciously since the League was categorical in its opposition to assimilation and the Board's policy based on it. Stan Davey, one of the founders of the League, who would go on to become secretary of the Federal Council for Aboriginal Advancement, made it clear that the assimilation policy of the Board was an abomination. He wrote:

> There are strong and real objections to an assimilation policy which assumes one of the races involved in the process has nothing to contribute to the national character and whose only hope is to 'get lost' in the dominant community. At no stage has the Australian Aborigine had the opportunity to voice his opinion as to the policy he would like to see. He has been told where his best interests lie and any claim to the right to maintain his identity, his culture, his possession of tribal lands or to participate in decisions as to his future relationships with other Australians have been completely denied.[7]

If Stan Davey, then the secretary of the Victorian Aborigines Advancement League, can write with such clarity about the position of Aboriginal people and the policies they have to deal with, why does the Neerim South Branch of the League honour speakers who refer to Aborigines as *wretched, unfortunate, downtrodden, demoralised* people whose 'lot must be improved'?[8] Underlying this language is the all-pervasive assumption of White superiority. Even Thomson uses it. As I look at many of the articles before me, I see that everyone speaks of Aborigines in this way. It is the language of the times. With the exception of Davey, who is able to find language that gives them the dignity they deserve, it seems most people can find no other way to articulate their concern about the *plight* of Aborigines. I shake my head, just as I know Pauline would. She has seen it all before, this strange and unconscious hypocrisy.

Except for the singing, which on first reading seems rather benign, none of these activities seemed to encroach upon the people at the Track. But a headline in the 23 September 1958 edition of the *Gazette* catches my eye: 'Aborigines to be Kept Out?' The article reports that Mr and Mrs W. H. Buchanan have offered the League a building block in Wood Street Drouin for a 'nominal sum' and 'a petition objecting that the presence of aboriginals in the residential area of Drouin would lower land values' has been circulated.[9] The Buchanans are named in Daryl's memoir. He says of them that they were connected with the church, although which church he had no clue nor did he care. He recalls that Mrs Buchanan came out to 'work her way into [the] lives' of the Track people by selling them cheap clothing she solicited through the local Radio Market, cleaned up and mended at her house before she brought them out. According to Daryl she, along with the other 'bible-bashers', would go 'from camp to camp talking about Jesus and Christian values... Always on the backs of the blackfellas trying to get them to improve their ways.'[10] That Daryl didn't like the Buchanans was obvious, and here they are in this article trying to organise housing for Aboriginal people. The article in *The Gazette* calls the Buchanans 'hard workers for the betterment of living conditions of Aborigines in the West Gippsland area'. I am suspicious. I know what will happen, that it will end in disaster, just as Daryl said; and here it is, the beginning of the dispossession, starting with the unconscious racism of well-meaning people – church people who have aligned themselves with the League.

And there is more. At the end of the same article, I see two sentences that catch me off guard: 'The League Branch is mainly responsible for the settlement of two aboriginal families west of Drouin, opposite the Drouin Racecourse. The Hood family has been living there for some time and, yesterday, the Rose family was moved from Jackson's Track at Jindivick to their new homes there.' I know the story, yet it stuns me to see it played out in these old papers. It is almost as if I have been hoping none of it were true.

I linger over those sentences for a long time. They state that Hoods and Roses were moved in 1958. This is almost four years before Daryl remembered the removal to have happened. Why was he so far out in his dates? What does this say about memory versus the Record? Of course, when he told his story to me, the old man had been remembering things he had not spoken about for more than forty years. Although he must have re-told the stories to himself over and over, trying to make sense of them over those years, it is clear he had re-shaped the stories to give them meaning in the present context of his life, which, when I met him, was pretty much one of loneliness and grief over lost happiness. Over the years he had altered the order of events.

Chronology in memory is always difficult. Memory compresses time. As he told me his story, Daryl was trying to work out when the removal had happened by connecting it with other events such as his brother's death, the sealing and straightening of the Track and the death of Roy Rose. He got it wrong largely because memory focuses on incidents in order of significance, thereby driving 'the oral recollection towards the figurative rather than the specific, to tropes rather than to facts'.[11] In Daryl's mind Stewart Hood, whose daughter, Euphie, was Daryl's wife, and who was responsible for the large extended family living at the Track – Daryl's family – was the Original Aboriginal Man. The removal of Stewart from the Track was a traumatic event for Daryl. It seems that he condensed several events into one, connecting Stewart's removal with another, later, mass removal associated with the very dramatic event of bulldozing the bark huts. This bulldozing symbolised for Daryl the dissolution of his family.

Neither Daryl nor I knew about the existence of the League when he was doing his remembering, and we never dreamed that the removal would have been publicised in the local papers. I am sure that if I had tried to dig deeper into the history of the event when I was working on Daryl's memoir, it would have done no good: had I attempted to verify every word of his story as he was telling it, the project would have come to a halt immediately. Daryl was on a knife edge speaking to me, always on the verge of pulling out of the whole process. Although I intuited what courage was involved in the telling of his story, I was pretty much in the dark when it came to understanding why he was so covert and almost frightened to tell it. And so I trod very lightly, doing my utmost to listen well and understand the meaning of the old man's words, the stuff that was coming out of his heart, rather than its accuracy in terms of the Record and of History.

In his book *Anzac memories*, Alastair Thomson writes of a similar experience he had when speaking with an old digger about his memories of being a soldier in Gallipoli during the Great War. He noticed that over time his subject became more articulate about what he remembered; early in the interview process, which lasted several years, his subject had been unable to express his memories about being fearful, but much later he was able to talk fluently about his fears. Thomson realised that over time the public narrative about war and heroism in general had changed such that 'what is possible to remember and articulate changes over time, and this can be attributed to shifts in personal identity and public attitudes'.[12] So with Daryl Tonkin. When I met him he thought he was a villain and a fool who had no reason or right to tell his story. Pauline managed to convince him that times had changed, that people were willing to listen to his tale and take it seriously. While I tended to dismiss his labelling himself a villain and a fool as a kind of false modesty, I understood that fears of racist rejection, along with fears of the law and 'the welfare', had rendered him and his Aboriginal family silent. The new genuine interest in, and hunger for, knowledge about Aborignes and Aboriginal history, empowered him to speak aloud those things that he had always thought should lie buried. As he and I worked together to find words with which to express his story, his confidence grew and he became more articulate. Nevertheless, to the very end he kept me from his family, especially, to my regret, from his beloved Euphie. He must have felt, deep in his heart, that telling his story to a stranger was a folly from which she needed to be protected.

Now here I am in the Historical Society, sitting amongst pages and pages of disintegrating yellow papers, wondering about what I have just discovered and how I feel about it. I decide that worrying about the chronology may be no more than a distraction in terms of understanding what happened and why; the truth is still there in both versions of the story. The Rose family 'was moved' and the League was 'mainly responsible for the settlement of two aboriginal families'. Just as Daryl said:

> A group of Christians [who] were white people didn't understand blackfellows [sic] ways and bush living. They dogged the blacks for years trying to change their ways and give up the bush... The blacks were told to get on the trucks and were taken to the block of land near Drouin... The Christians had wrecked the blackfellows [sic] lifes [sic]...[13]

Daryl's story is the same as the Record, even if there is a discrepancy in dates, but his version gives it a narrative shape that includes subtext from the heart. Perhaps more importantly, it takes a completely different point of view from the Record. The Record tells the official view, the view of the perpetrators; Daryl's memoir tells the view of the victim. It tells the side of the story that usually remains untold and off the record. I must remember that and measure both views against the other.

I finally decide, after trying to think all this through, that all I can feel is the cold in this old dark reading room in the Historical Society. I am surrounded by photos on the walls that remember and celebrate men whose voices, attitudes and assumptions fill the documents in the Archive, images that represent progress on the frontier: photos of the great mountain ash forests that once surrounded this little town but were so proudly cleared away to make room for dairy cows and their pasture; photos of moustachioed men in shirt sleeves outside the first pub; more of men in coats and waistcoats with watch chains and cravats standing on their stovepipe legs in thick woollen pants, arms crossed over their chests. Where are the voices of the Stewart Hoods and the Pauline Mulletts? Why aren't their pictures here on these walls? It all makes me angry.

White and moustachioed: important White men's portraits hang on the walls at the Historical Society
Photo by the author

    I close the grey cardboard-bound folio of papers for the year 1958 and take it back to its home in a large walk-in safe in one of the darker rooms in the building. On the shelves inside this vault papers dating back far into the nineteenth century are stacked higgledy-piggledy as high as the ceiling. To enter I must use a long, old key, turning it in the lock just so before a brass handle clicks and the heavy safe door swings open, revealing the stacks inside. I have fossicked through these stacks looking for traces, clues, artefacts that prove the dead were once living. The papers I have perused include *The Guardian,* which first reported to the people of Gippsland the doings of Angus McMillan, parliamentarian and protector of Aborigines, but neglected to mention that in his youth he was an organiser of the Highland Brigade. The Highland Brigade may have been responsible for a massacre of the Brataualong, Pauline's direct ancestors, at Warrigal creek in 1843. 'Everyone in Gippsland knew of the Massacre',[14] according to historian Don Watson who grew up in Gippsland. No, I think, not all the lives of the dead are in these papers.

The Archive's collection of newspapers
Photo by Larry Hills

I feel too cold and sad to go on looking, but as I place the folio back on the stack and prepare to lock the safe door, I realise I can also feel Pauline watching me. She is giving me no clues about what to think or feel; she simply watches. She is waiting for me to figure it out. She knows there is more to the story than I see, that there is more to her father's fear than I understand. I can't tell if her expression is dark, frowning with frustration at my obtuseness or if there is a twinkle in her eye as she watches me get closer, closer, but not quite there yet. I have seen that expression many times when her eyes are laughing and her lips are ready to part into a broad smile as I finally see the light and get what she has been trying to tell me. I feel that if I turn the key in the lock and walk away, I might never see the light. I cannot risk having that lively expression of Pauline's close down and go blank. It might break my heart.

Instead of closing the door, I put the key in my pocket and go back to take another volume of the *Gazette* from the stack, and then another, until I find it all. In June 1959, it is reported that four families have been moved to houses in the district, but it does not say where. It does say that 'there are fifteen children in the four families and the League is keen to see them have opportunities for schooling as other children have'.[15] I wonder if it is the Austins that are being referred to. I take note of the comment about opportunities for schooling. It doesn't square with what I know: according to Daryl, the kids at the Track, Austins' kids in particular, attended Labortouche Primary and had a wonderful teacher. I also wonder what is meant by 'as other children'. I know this is a direct quote from Alwyn Jensen, the most energetic of the League members. Is it an assumption that

Aboriginal children want to be like other children? Is it an assimilationist comment? Perhaps it is just a throw-away line that comes out of the unconscious mind of a man who assumes his way is superior to that of the wretched Aborigines he feels compassion for.

Courtesy of Museum Victoria: Registration No. XP 1679. Photographer: Richard Seeger

Children at Jackson's Track
Reproduced with permission also from Regina Rose

I come across a report, dated August 1959, about the activities of the League. It may have been written by the secretary of the Neerim Branch of the League, Mr W. A. Knowles, or by the the president, Mr A. Jensen. It reads 'All known aborigines in the Warragul-Drouin area were housed in decent dwellings and provided with some furniture'.[16] This surprises me. Daryl remembered that there were only two small shacks where Hoods and Roses moved to. According to him, the rest of the housing, if that's what it could be called, was made up of tents and maybe a run-down caravan. And what did 'known aborigines' mean? Was it assumed that there were many more who were unknown?

In January 1960 Mr Jensen writes an angry letter to the editor registering 'the strongest protest against the unreasonable attitude shown by Cr Stoll [of the Buln Buln Shire

Council]'.[17] Stoll had complained long and loud in a Council meeting about the risk that drunken 'aborigines' would make a public nuisance of themselves if they were to move into town. Jensen calls Mr Stoll *ignorant, dishonest, prejudiced*. He calls the 'dark folk' *decent*.

In August 1960 there is a report about a new £3000 home being built for Mrs Violet Harrison, an Aboriginal woman with nine children. The State CWA donated £1500 from their Thanksgiving Fund and the Aborigines Welfare Board the rest. The entire project was originated by Mrs Buchanan from the League.[18] So, I think, the Board and the League were working together in the West Gippsland area. How could that be when the League was begun as a guard against the activities of the Board?

I cannot find the answer in these old newspapers. I have reached the end of any references to moving people into houses. There is plenty of activity concerning arrangements at the houses and the helping hands lent by League members to build a kitchen, put on the water, start a garden. There is report of holding 'fellowship meetings' for the people at the so called 'settlement' once a week, and educational meetings for the general community on a regular basis. At one point, missionaries from the Aborigines Island Mission of Australia held services at the home of Mrs Hood at the 'settlement'. The Presbyterian Men's Brotherhood decides to 'adopt' an Aborigine. But there is nothing more about housing. I will have to go to the National Archives to find out more about the Board and its connection to the League in our area.

As I put the last folio of papers back in the stacks, slowly close the heavy door and turn the key, I think to myself that I know more about the details of Daryl's story than he does now. He was not aware of the existence of the League, and most likely still isn't. He knew Doug Nicholls very well, even staying at his house next to the footy grounds in Fitzroy a number of times, and he consented to let him to hold services at the Track whenever the weather was fine. Of course Daryl knew that Nicholls was a pastor, after all he was called Pastor Doug at the Track. But he did not know that Nicholls was Field Officer for the League and that the other Christians who Daryl thought were plaguing the blackfellas were also members of a branch of the League and well-known to Nicholls. If he had known about the group fighting for Aboriginal rights, would he have joined them or would he have stood up against them? If he had known who they were, is it possible he may have understood why Stewart Hood was not afraid of them and had even argued that he thought they were good people with good ideas?[19]

The sad irony is that the Aborigines Welfare Board on the one hand and the Aborigines' Advancement League on the other emerged at almost exactly the same time that

Jackson's Track, which for years had been no more than a boggy winding one-lane track with 'pot holes big enough to bury a cow in',[20] was straightened and sealed by the Shire Council. The new road made its way through the Aboriginal camps that had existed, peacefully hidden there, for seventeen years. Also, in 1957 Daryl Tonkin's brother Harry died, and his sister Mavis made an attempt to wrest the timber mill and the land from Daryl as an expression of her disapproval of his relationship with Euphemia Hood Mullett and the rest of the Aboriginal people camped at Jackson's Track. Mavis did her utmost to undermine the business and caused work to come to a temporary standstill before Daryl struggled back to his feet. These events left the families at the Track vulnerable to the machinations and influence of the Board, the League, and as it turned out, religious zealotry. Daryl Tonkin was only partially aware of this convergence of events.

It's late. As I slowly back out of the Historical Society locking one door after another, all with different oddly shaped keys, possibly the same keys handled by the Shire Officers who walked these corridors in the 1890s, I think of Pauline. She is not just watching me here; she is guiding me. Right now she is patiently waiting to see if I will finally get to the place she wants me to be. Maybe she thinks all this searching is preliminary, a prerequisite to real knowledge. I know she does not yet trust the importance of what I am finding. Is it taking me towards the truth, or at least towards some sort of resolution?

ENDNOTES

1   Anonymous (1985, p. 52).

2   Anonymous (1985, p. 52).

3   McLean, Charles. Report Upon the Operation of the Aborigines Act 1928 and the Regulations and Order made Thereunder, Melbourne, 1957, B408.

4   Anonymous (1985, p. 53).

5   Warragul Gazette, 'Plea for Better Deal for Aborigines', 10 October 1957, p. 4.

6   Warragul Gazette, 'Warragul Meets Leader of expedition to Binidbu Tribe', 15 July 1958, p. 12; and 'Ashamed of our treatment of aborigines' 22 July 1958, p. 18.

7   Stan Davey (1963).

8   Warragul Gazette, 10 October 1957, p. 4; and 'Aborigines Sing at Warragul Meeting' 26 August 1958, p. 19.

9   Warragul Gazette, 'Aborigines to be kept out?' 23 September 1958, p. 1.

10   Landon and Tonkin (1999, p. 252).

11   John Murphy (1986, pp. 164–165).

[12] Alastair Thomson (1994, p. 237).

[13] Landon and Tonkin (1999).

[14] Don Watson (1984, p. 167).

[15] Warragul Gazette, 'Housing for Aborigines,' 9 June 1959, p. 11.

[16] Warragul Gazette, 'District League has Done Much to Advance Welfare for Aborigines,' 4 August 1959, p. 19.

[17] Warragul Gazette, 'This is what our Reader's Think: League's Protest,' 12 January 1960, p. 7.

[18] Warragul Gazette, 'New Home for Aborigines,' 2 Aug 1960, p. 1.

[19] Landon and Tonkin (1999, p. 251).

[20] Landon and Tonkin (1999, p. 7).

REFERENCES

Anonymous. 1985. *Victims or victors? The story of the Victorian Aborigines Advancement League.* Melbourne: Hyland House Publishing.

Davey, Stan. 1963. 'Genesis or genocide? The Aboriginal assimilation policy'. *Provocative pamphlets* 101 (July 1963). Available from: http://www.mun.ca/rels/restmov/texts/pp/PP101.HTM.

Landon, Carolyn; Tonkin, Daryl. 1999. *Jackson's Track: Memoir of a Dreamtime place.* Melbourne: Penguin.

Murphy, John. 1986. 'The voice of memory: History, autobiography and oral memory'. *Historical studies* 22 (87): 157–175.

Thomson, Alastair. 1994. *Anzac memories: Memory and wartime bereavement in Australia.* Melbourne: Melbourne University Press.

Watson, Don. 1984. *Caledonia Australis: Scottish highlanders on the frontier of Australia.* Sydney: Collins.

Cite this chapter as: Landon, Carolyn. 2006. 'The story of the League'. In *Jackson's Track revisited: History, remembrance and reconciliation.* Melbourne: Monash University ePress. pp. 4.1–4.14. DOI: 10.2104/jtr06004.

CHAPTER 5

MR JENSEN'S STORY

Carolyn Landon

This chapter explores the heart and mind of a 'do-gooder' in the era of assimilation, through historical records and through oral testimony. Alwyn Jensen, a key figure of *Jackson's Track*, emerges as an authoritative and energetic controller. Jensen, the main focus of Daryl Tonkin's wrath, was Secretary of the Local Committee of the Aborigines Welfare Board, and President of the Neerim Branch of the Victorian Aborigines Advancement League. Foremost, however, was his mission to establish a church among the Aboriginal people at Jackson's Track. This chapter also reflects on oral history, which is is predicated on active human relationships between historians and their sources. The historian must expand the imagination to encompass two views that are often divergent – that of the teller and that of the listener.

Although the archives in the Warragul Historical Society make it clear that the Aborigines Welfare Board and the Victorian Aborigines Advancement League were entangled in their involvement with the Jackson's Track people as early as 1959, documents in the National Archives show that it does not become an official arrangement until October 1962. Interesting: 1962 is the year Daryl nominated in his memoir for the occurrence of tragic events. A press statement from the office of the Chief Secretary of Victoria, The Honourable Sir Arthur Rylah, announced the appointment of members of the Neerim Branch of the League to the Local Committee for the Board.[1] Members included representatives from the Buln Buln Shire Council and the Drouin Police, the Health Inspector, as well as the 'do-gooders' mentioned in Daryl's memoir: 'Mr A. H. Jensen, (farmer) of Neerim South, who is president of the local branch of the Aborigines Advancement League; Mrs P. V. Buchanan of Drouin who is an active worker for aboriginal welfare in the district; Mr H. T. Cowden (farmer) of Neerim South who is an active member of the Aborigines Advancement League.' This Local Committee was the third of its kind, according to the statement, 'appointed under the provisions of the Aborigines Act. Other committees are functioning in Warnambool and Morwell.' The duties of the new members were to 'assist and advise the Aborigines Welfare Board on matters concerning the welfare and assimilation of aborigine'.[2] There it was. *Assimilation*. The members were to assist with assimilation. This seems a conflict of interest.

It also seems that Mr Jensen was aware of the conflict, for it is noted by Mr P. E. Felton, Regional Superintendent of Aborigines Welfare, that the League members nominated for the Local Committee 'do not see eye to eye with the rest of the Aborigines

Advancement League and are strictly concerned with the local issues. They have a slight doubt that they may not see eye to eye with the Board on certain issues, but we have endeavoured to reassure them...'[3]

The Archive says nothing more about why the people in the Neerim Branch of League were troubled with the central body, nor does it say what troubles them about the Board. Of course, that blank space can be filled in with conjecture, an educated, and probably fairly accurate, guess; instead I decide it's time to find the members of the League that Janet Cowden told me about who are still alive and ask what they remember. Janet puts me on to her sister Flo Cowden White, who was her father's 'little mate' when she was small and who remembers accompanying him on visits to the Aboriginal people at the Track and later at the Camp or Settlement on the highway.

The Cowden family: Florence, Elizabeth, Janet and John with their parents Hector and Ina
Photo courtesy of Janet Cowden

She also tells me how to contact Alwyn Jensen. In all the mixture of information gathered – the articles and documents in the Historical Society, the National Archives, Cowden's papers, and Daryl's memoir – Jensen is the one who emerges as the mover and shaker, the most authoritative, the most in control. His name comes up more than any other: not only was he the main focus of Daryl Tonkin's wrath, he was also Secretary of the Local Committee of the Aborigines Welfare Board, and President of the Neerim Branch of the League after Bert Clarke left the area.

I am pleased and surprised that Jensen is eager to tell his story, in spite of the negative role he played in Daryl's published memoir. However, because oral history is predicated on active human relationships between historians and their sources,[4] I am worried about what kind of rapport I will have with him: I am known as Daryl's co-author and I have already begun to draw conclusions about Jensen's activities and his attitudes from the documents I have read and the words Daryl and I have written about him. If I am to get Jensen to document for me the personal meaning of his experience, albeit in a short interview, I must try to conquer my prejudices and find a way to ease tension that might exist between us. When I finally do meet him, his down-to-earth congeniality makes me realise the apprehension is in me more than it is in him. I wonder why he does not feel the same, but it becomes clear as he begins his testimony that he seems supremely confident in the rightness of his 'doings', whatever they are. The interview is conducted as a conversation. Before we start I show him some of my research to let him know that some of his activities during that period have been documented.

I feel I am in a familiar place when I hear Mr Jensen begin to use a vernacular that is similar to that used by Daryl, his contemporary. He swings into telling yarns as easily as Daryl. His is the authentic voice of a man born just after the Great War, when Australia was beginning to identify itself as a unique place where mateship, community spirit, and a broadly positive outlook was the norm. His words reveal his faith in the Anglo-Celtic work ethic and his stories are filled with practical solutions to difficult problems. When I listen to his resonant voice constructing his narrative, I am reminded that Jensen is a lay preacher. Much of what he says is structured like a sermon: an anecdote followed by a moral to close the lesson. He develops character, re-constructs dialogue, fills-in details of time and place to deepen the impact of his account and give it meaning. I am mesmerised by his stories for they reveal how it felt to be mixing it with the Aborigines Welfare Board and the League in the forest at Jackson's Track.

Although my questions and constant referral to Daryl's memoir dredge up memories Jensen may have buried, it emerges that his idea of the place of Aboriginal people in Australian society has not changed over forty years. Like Daryl, Alwyn Jensen is a rare character in that he is absolutely authentic, an artefact, so to speak; he is a man who grew up in the era of protection and was most active in the era of assimilation; he does not seem interested in the changed public (or social) attitude that exists in 2006, although he derives some satisfaction from the fact that people are now involved in the 'Aboriginal issue' when, throughout his entire lifetime, it was shrouded in the 'Great Australian Silence'.[5] I realise that while I am speaking with him it is important I keep in mind that my own context is very different from his. I must always consider his point of view, understand that his way of assessing and understanding his life experience must be taken seriously.[6] I must expand my imagination to encompass these two divergent views – his and mine.

Hector Cowden's daughter is also willing to be interviewed. Compared to Mr Jensen, Flo Cowden White is a minimalist. Her comments are thoughtful, deeply considered and carefully expressed. She is mindful of protecting her father's and her family's dignity throughout her interview. Like Jensen, she also feels morally bound to be as honest as she can, and so doesn't shirk from difficult subjects. As she speaks, it is clear she is reconstructing memories she has rarely visited and, seeing them from the point of view of an adult for the first time, she is fitting them together in such a way as to reach new conclusions about what was actually going on back in the 1950s. Flo is my contemporary and an acquaintance; we sat on the same Primary School Council together. I had no idea of her connection to Hector Cowden until Janet told me of it, but I know Flo to be an avid reader, and I realise she is in tune with and in sympathy with contemporary issues. Because she is talking about her father and her childhood experiences, she too will have to expand her imagination to encompass divergent views – those of her father in her remembered past and those that she now holds in her reconsidered present. It turns out Flo's testimony is almost like an antidote to that of Jensen, who does not seem to feel he needs to reassess or draw new conclusions about the past.

Alas, because she has died, the only access I have to Mrs Buchanan, the third member of both the Local Committee and the League, is through the memory of others. Alwyn Jensen remembers her well and it turns out he is willing to talk freely about her. Dot Mullett, Pauline's half-sister, also remembers 'Aunty Pen' and is able to paint a colourful picture of a woman whose warm-hearted nature made her beloved by the children. "Uncle Bill and Aunty Pen," Dot laughs with delight as she remembers the Buchanans. "He was a big tall fellow and she was just a little short woman. We were taller than her when we were just kids."[7]

Religion was the most obvious factor that made the local Committee members feel they were different from the central bodies of both the Board and League. All three of them – Mrs Buchanan, Mr Jensen and Mr Cowden – were evangelists connected to the Methodist and Presbyterian churches.[8] Flo White, who is deeply religious, as all the Cowden family seem to be, remembers going to the Track with her father to take furniture, clothes and bedding to the 'unfortunate folk'[9] there. She says of her father, "I think it would be easiest to say that he was trying to demonstrate God's love by giving of himself when he had very little to give... I think that's what our relationship with God requires us to do, to share."

Mr Jensen freely describes his conversion in 1956:

> My input into Aborigines was not just to better them physically and financially. That was part of it. My idea was spiritual. I had this conversion and six weeks after God called me to Aborigines. I went to a meeting in the hall here with Pastor Doug Nicholls and I was walking out and a voice said to me, 'I want you to work with Aborigines.' And I laughed just like Sarah did when God said, 'you'll have a child'... I forgot all about it for a fortnight until Aunty Pen [Buchanan]... she must have heard that I had made a commitment and she came to me and said, 'Mr Jensen, are you interested in Aborigines?' And from then on I became very interested... My aim was to let them know that Jesus loved them, that He died for them and that they would go to Heaven when they died if they changed their ways and followed Him. That was basically it.[10]

Jensen, Buchanan and Cowden had walked amongst the Aboriginal people at Jackson's Track before the Board or League existed. Because of their religious affiliations, their primary purpose was to 'uplift' the 'folk'.

Remembering the past and reconstructing it in the present as she is doing, Flo White recognises that which she is sure her father did not: "that the Aboriginal folk did have a spiritual life and," she continues somewhat cryptically, "that there were factors to be taken into account and places to be tread lightly." I understand her to mean that there was no lightness in the approach of these do-gooders to the people at the Track. Jensen says, after some prompting, that he thinks maybe he should have asked the Aboriginal people about their own spiritual world, but he falls straight into the attitudes of the times when he follows that admission with, "they were westernised as much as they could be as far as I was concerned and as far as their culture went... as far as their culture and their religion... well, not religion as such... I don't think there was much there."

He seems to have accepted the contemporary notion that the Aboriginal people of south-eastern Australia were in a stage of transition between the old ways and the new and that to bring up the old ways as if they were legitimate might slow down the transition.[11] More to the point he believed there was no culture or faith left in them to which they could adhere.

He says over and over again:

> All I wanted to do was to present to them the experience I had had in the Lord because it is available to all of them... I felt that I had been saved from darkness, from hell and I wanted them to have the same opportunity because I could see that even though they had been through Lake Tyers [where they would have been introduced to Christianity through the Anglican Church] I knew they hadn't had the experience of the Lord.

This purpose must have given him a great sense of authority – the authority of the Lord. He recalls that at one point he turned up at the settlement on the highway to conduct a fellowship meeting, as he called his religious services, and Mrs Dora Hood, Pauline's grandmother, was distraught because one of the men had gone wild and locked everyone out of the house. Jensen approached the house:

> And so I went in there. I had my Bible in my hand and called him by name 'What's the problem?' And he talked quietly and I said, 'I wonder if you'd go somewhere else while we had the meeting?' And he said, 'All right, Mr Jensen.' I think because I had my Bible in my hand, he recognised Who I was representing.

Jensen must have been an imposing figure, tall and lanky and serious, always with his Bible in his hand, always ready to witness to the love of God. When I suggest the people may have been responding to him as they would a mission manager, he readily agrees.

> Yes, that's right. It may not have been me personally, but it was because they knew what I was representing. Quite a few of them did respect us, I think. I hope so.

His religious mission extended beyond the fellowship meetings. The meetings of Neerim Branch of the League, of which Jensen became president, were opened and closed with prayer. In addressing a report to the members, Jensen begins with, 'Praise goes to God for His all sufficiency; my Grace is sufficient for Thee.'[12] At least once, these religious overtones served to exclude people who might have become involved with the group and might have helped it to balance its local activities. Jensen remembers that well-respected local humanist and left-wing thinker Dr Allen McPhate soon left the group because, as Jensen says, "he wasn't interested in the spiritual side of things… we'd run it on a more or less spiritual basis, you know, opening with prayer and a short reading." This religious element was a strong motivator. Jensen said:

> You have to express your faith by works. In the Bible it says, 'faith without works is dead', but you're not saved by your works. Faith first and then the evidence of your faith is what you do in relationship to that faith.

It is noticed by researchers and academics that the 'Aboriginal cause' often attracted people who were 'singular men and women',[13] many of whom were avowed Christians whose missionary zeal was nurtured by the Church. It is certainly true of Buchanan, Cowden and Jensen that their religious fervour gave them the courage to stand up before a conservative and, according to Jensen, 'ninety percent racist' community and speak out on behalf of Aboriginals. By saying that ninety percent of the community was racist, Jensen is implying that he and the others were in a small minority. This seems to be a point of honour with him and it emphasises his commitment to righting wrongs done to Aboriginal people. In this he showed abundant energy in arguing with the Shire Councillors, soliciting charity from their respective congregations, writing articles on their activities for the local papers, and letters of complaint or anger to the editor.

The archive documents suggest that Jensen was a man who was active in many ways in the community and seemed to be well-known and mostly well-respected because he took his responsibilities seriously and could always be counted on to pull his weight for whatever committee he was on. He was a natural leader. He confirms this when he talks about his extensive work in the Church: "I was taking up to three services of a Sunday here in my own [Methodist] church and Sunday School and I had other involvements: the Gideons and I was secretary of the convention, and there was a ministry in Warragul…"

Alwyn Jensen
Photo courtesy of Alwyn Jensen

One of his main purposes in going amongst the people at the Track was to begin his own church there. He writes:

> I went to Jackson's Track in response to Jesus' last command, 'Go into all the world and preach the gospel to every creature' (Mark chapter 6 verse 15 KJV)... I had hoped a little church fellowship meeting might develop, as they enjoyed the programs I shared with them over many years... The Aborigines Inland Mission, with head quarters in Sydney, came to help with four aboriginal [*sic*] men. They came in different times over two or three years and got on well with the people, as they had been brought up in similar situations.[14]

Hector Cowden was well known for his singularity. He worked independently of any church, although he had belonged to the Presbyterian Church before he was asked to leave for standing up to the minister and accusing him of misrepresenting the true word of God. He had been a Sunday-school teacher and a member of the Brotherhood, a Presbyterian Bible study group, but upon leaving the church became individualistic and, judging by reactions from some of his still-living contemporaries when his name is mentioned, slightly unconventional – even, to non-believers, slightly confrontational – in his activities: he was a very strong-minded man whose belief had to be proclaimed. Some of his energy went into maintaining what his daughter calls the 'roadside pulpit', a billboard upon which he posted notices about God, texts from the Bible, and opinions about wayfarers.

Mrs Buchanan, or Aunty Pen, as everyone called her, was, on the other hand, a kind-hearted, generous person who was guided her whole life by the hand of God. Her purpose in life was to do good works and take in the wretched and the poor. It was she who brought Alwyn Jensen to Jackson's Track for the first time after she had been told about the commandment he had received from the Lord. "Now, I would have been a long time getting their [the Aborigines'] confidence," says Mr Jensen, "but they accepted me almost immediately because she took me and told me what it was all about."

She often had the Aboriginal children stay with her for weeks on end and, according to Dot Mullett, the kids loved it because they thought it was a holiday: "We had to say grace and prayers and use our fork and spoon properly and have a shower every day before we went to school. It was something new for us. We thought it was fun because we never had that sort of thing on the Track."[15]

This undying faith and spreading of the Word by Jensen, Buchanan and Cowden, underpinned by the assumptions of the times – a mixture of the need for protection and assimilation – was, in Daryl Tonkin's eyes, catastrophic for the people from the Track. But Daryl was wrong. It wasn't the religion that caused a catastrophe.

It must be said that right from the beginning of the interview, Jensen protests that he did not disapprove of the way the people at the Track lived. And both of Cowden's daughters insist that their father felt the same way. They point out that, like Jensen, he 'lived in circumstances not much flasher in his early years'. But there seems to be a lapse in continuity here. If these statements are true then why did Jensen and Cowden think they needed to improve the conditions of the Aboriginals?

"[While] the object was a spiritual one, I wanted to better their physical life, too. I believe that was an outworking of the spirit of God," says Jensen. Cowden was of a similar mind-set. His daughter says that he would have been unhappy to see folk living in poor circumstances when there was so much prosperity on their doorstep. All three do-gooders took the people at the Track under their wings and spent time and energy clothing, furnishing and feeding their charges. Jensen, who considered that the people were starving when he first came upon them, says that he brought them loaves of bread donated from the local baker and passed them out to the people. He and Mrs Buchanan advertised on the local Radio Market and other concerned people in the district donated more things than could be managed. Cowden spent much time in his truck, as did Jensen, carting furniture to the huts on the Track. Eventually they began to worry about what such largesse might do to the morality of their charges. "We could see that what we were doing was wrong, too. Well, right in one sense and wrong in another. It was making them dependent on gifts," says Jensen. So they began to teach the Aborigines thrift by charging them five pence for each piece of clothing. The money would go to the hospital to benefit the Aborigines when they needed medical attention. It was a righteous thing to do.

If these statements approving of the way of life of people at the Track are true, wouldn't it have been likely that neither Jensen nor Cowden would have anything to do with convincing people to move off the property? Wouldn't they have continued to spend their energies improving the living conditions of the people and preaching the Word to them? Why, then, did they become involved with the Board and what was it they disagreed with? Jensen seems to have had two reasons for his involvement. "I knew I would have to go with the Board or get out of it," he says. As he was unwilling to give up his mission with the Aborigines, he felt he had to find a way of cooperating with the Board. Later, he writes:

> It was not my intention to try to rehouse the families, but to help them in their situations and I believe I did this. When Mr. Davey, the housing member of the AWB [the Aborigines Welfare Board] and the Victorian Housing Commissioner, told me that they were going to assimilate all aboriginals [sic] I contested the idea, but he was adamant. After some thought, I agreed to help and kept in contact with the Housing Commissioner.[16]

What was it about the assimilation he contested? Jensen explained:

> Putting the people in houses in the city and not giving them any... I mean bringing them from the bush... I was brought up in the bush and lived in not much better condition than they did sometimes during the depression years, and I know what it was like to come into a powered house with hot water. You know, you're all at sea. But this was my objection to it.

He also thought it cruel to move people off Lake Tyers Mission Station into towns. Yet he did know that housing them was inevitable. In his practical way, he devised a plan. "It was my idea to get them a house not totally isolated, but isolated from neighbours," he said, "but in the town, and Rokeby – and here at Neerim South – was just ideal. Right out of the town but right close to it. It would be a training… a good home, but it was within the township but no neighbours next door to worry them."

This was in keeping with the League's policy of improvement of housing and living standards. I reminded myself, they weren't working with the Board at first. The League came first, then the Board. But before that it was purely the Christianity of these people that motivated their actions. In 1957, while McLean was still gathering data for his report and before the League was formed, Jensen signed the Aboriginal people up for 'the Social', as he calls it. How did he know that the status of Victorian Aborigines had changed such that they finally had the right to vote in local elections and were eligible for social security benefits? Did Bert Clarke tell him? Did he learn it from the Buln Buln Shire Council? He tells me he saw a public notice about new citizen rights in 1956. "That's how I knew." Perhaps this understanding of bureaucratic systems is part of what made Jensen the leader in this group of good people with good intentions. Is he the one who eventually led people to the Board? Jensen describes what happened when he signed the Aboriginal people up for 'the Social':

> One of my first jobs was – I don't know if it was the right thing to do – was to get them on social welfare… entitlement to it. So, I filled in the forms for them. I wondered later whether it was a wise move because the fellas used to get it and drink it away, although they used to buy food with it. The Dows brought theirs to us – to Hilda [Jensen's wife] – and asked would she handle the Social money, dish it out for food, but, oh, they were getting something like £5 a week and Joycie expected to pay the rent, clothes, money to spare. It was getting Hilda down a bit, so… She did that for a while but, oh, I don't think they knew what it was then.

As Jensen says, he didn't know if signing the people up for social security benefits was the right thing to do because, almost immediately, it seemed to have a detrimental effect. Jensen found himself in a situation where he was handling their money – his wife doing the shopping for them – and their reliance on him was redoubling. This must have been the opposite of what he wanted. He was trying to give the people independence, but they became more dependent. He found himself responsible for their lives. Did he want such responsibility and the control that came with it? His tone and the way he shapes this anecdote indicate that he thought it was inevitable. In his memoir Daryl stressed with pride that the 'Welfare', as he called it, never had anything to do with, nor had any hold over, the people on his property. With one gesture Jensen inadvertently destroyed this independence of which Daryl was so proud. And Daryl saw it. It seems that Jensen saw it, too, but the damage was done.

Alwyn with Hilda
Photo courtesy of Alwyn Jensen

Essentially, Jensen and company found themselves becoming paternalistic towards their charges. As per the times and perhaps because people like the Dows and Austins, who had come off the mission at Lake Tyers, demonstrated such willingness to be taken care of, they found their interaction with the Aboriginal people like that of adults with children. Jensen thought they were wonderful people with marvellous senses of humour, but considered that he needed to be on call to answer their every need. He says he worked about thirty hours a week for their good. His own work suffered for it.

Yes, well it was a bit awkward. I was putting thirty hours a week into
Aboriginals for the first twelve months. And I was trying to run a

farm, and what I did, I employed a chap, who I couldn't afford really, but the Lord saw me out. He would milk of a night... he'd help me of a morning and then I'd give him jobs to do in the day while I went away and then he'd milk at night... We got by. But the farm didn't show any improvement; I had to do a lot of work after that to catch up.

Jensen found himself on call twenty-four hours a day. He tells me several stories about going into the houses and placating abusive men. Once, when a fellow named Jacky Green was being particularly loud and threatening, Jensen was called and, as he tells it:

So, I went in and I said, 'How ya going, Jacky?' and of course Jacky was a returned man and he knew I was, too. 'Oh, Al, old pal!' and he put his arm around me, 'We won the war, didn't we?' and we just walked out. And away he went. I didn't hear anything more about that, but that was their attitude. They weren't abusive to me at all.

At times he would have whole families bedded down in his lounge room and would dispense tea and a warm breakfast in the morning before he sent them on their way. Jensen's wife was even called upon to deliver a baby, which wouldn't wait for Jensen to get its mother to the hospital in the truck. "She went down and did what was necessary," Jensen said of his wife.

Cowden's view was possibly also protectionist, by then an old fashioned attitude that had been replaced by assimilation. He thought that if people needed to be moved from the Track they should go back to Lake Tyers where there was already an established settlement. His protectionist views may have made him more sensitive than others to idea that the group of Aboriginal families at Jackson's Track functioned as a community and therefore shouldn't be broken up, but by this time Bert Clarke had established the Neerim Branch of the League which had begun to agitate for better living conditions for Aborigines throughout the state. Ironically it was the activities of Jensen, Cowden and Buchanan on the Track that brought these three souls to the League, and it was their connection with the League that brought the attention of the Board to the existence of the large number of Aborigines living in Police District D, a fact that until then had been completely unknown to Police Superintendent Richards and Charles McLean. As Jensen sees it, it was the Board that showed the least respect and eventually caused the most trouble.

The young Hector Cowden
Photo courtesy of Janet Cowden

The oral testimonies of Jensen and Cowden's daughter reveal a part of the history of the Track that the Archive leaves empty. Chronology is sometimes confused and incidents compressed and, consciously or unconsciously, given symbolic meaning. The value of the narratives lies in the way that the human heart, the ego, and the subconscious paint a picture of real people of courage and conviction battling their demons and confusion, their blindness and prejudices, in order to do something right and good in their world. In the Archive we find evidence of Jensen's sense of responsibility and the weight with which he sometimes carried it: he complains at one point in a letter to Mr Felton at the Board that 'all this type of work is left to me'.[17] This last comment is in connection with the move of some of the Track families onto a five-acre paddock just outside Drouin on the highway, near the race track. The place had been donated by a friend of Mrs Buchanan for the folk from the Track. Jensen and the other League members called it 'the Settlement'. The Archive helps us to set straight Jensen's chronology and adds detail to the list of things he has forgotten to include, but it gives us little of his heart, unlike his testimony. We can see none of Cowden in the Archives and only a little of him in the papers he left behind because, as his daughter says, "[When] we discovered his papers, we found he had burned quite a bit of his archive, but we don't know why. Why did he keep what he had kept? It is interesting." It seemed he was determined to bury his deeper, more passionate self with him when he died, but Flo White's testimony has revealed a thoughtful, profound and avid believer who 'fell to his knees and prayed with tears in his eyes when he saw what a failure his work with the Aboriginal people had been' after they had been shifted into town.

Although he dedicated a good part of fourteen years to their well-being, Jensen indicated that he felt frustrated that life did not seem to improve for the Aboriginal people. He writes in a letter to Harry Davey that 'drunkenness and overcrowding is back in Drouin… I am still holding weekly gospel meetings… but see little result.'[18] At the end of the interview, he says to me:

> My interest waned after about… for thirteen years I maintained the witness… I believe that God closed the door for me in taking a church to the Aborigines… It finished up it was only Ma Hood and I were there and I went for quite a long time for her because she needed encouragement, but the others had been shifted into homes. There were two, three in Warragul, some in Drouin and they weren't interested in getting together.

On my way home from Neerim South after my talk with Jensen, I think about his answer to one of the mysteries that still exists in Daryl's story. And that is, who bulldozed the houses in which the Aboriginal people lived at Jackson's Track for more than twenty years? Two years earlier, when Janet showed me her father's papers, I had become curious about what kind of man Hector Cowden was. I asked her what her father did. She had answered that he was a bulldozer driver. I was amazed at her answer, pondered it for many days and finally asked her, "Was it your father who bulldozed the huts?" She had been shocked at the thought and said unequivocally, "No." When I asked Mr Jensen who bulldozed the huts he said:

> I think that was the Board. I don't think it was the League. I didn't have any involvement in it. I don't even know who did the work. No, I had no knowledge that it was even happening.

I am disappointed by this answer for I can find no documentation that shows the Board had anything to do with it. The bulldozing of the huts is a symbolic act in Daryl's memoir, yet I can find no one to take responsibility for it. I must keep asking and looking.

Later, when I look over the notes and transcript of Jensen's testimony I focus on something he said in the middle of the conversation when I mentioned Daryl Tonkin:

> I never met Daryl Tonkin… I don't know, but this is what I have
> imagined. Daryl Tonkin must have had great concern for that family
> – for Euphie – otherwise he wouldn't have taken her in. He must have
> helped the Roses a fair bit. Here's a bloke comes in and takes over his
> little bit. That's how I imagined he may have seen me because I didn't
> know he was doing much for them at that time. But it wouldn't have
> mattered. I was still going to do something because to me they seemed
> to be in poverty conditions.

The words 'otherwise he wouldn't have taken her in' in reference to Daryl's relationship with Euphie Hood Mullett needled me when he said them. Did they mean that Jensen did not want to acknowledge that Daryl Tonkin, a White man, could fall in love with a Black woman, take her as his wife and be loyal and faithful to her? During the interview I defined Daryl's relationship with Euphie and told Jensen they had had nine children together.

"He considered himself married to Euphie even though he didn't go to a church. He was loyal to her…" I said. "Oh, yes, he did the right thing," he replied. "Oh, yeah, I appreciated him for that." At first I didn't know why he used those words in his reply. Now, when I review '…he did the right thing' in my mind I begin to realise what it means. This phrase is part of the vernacular of the 1950s. A man marries a woman if she gets pregnant. That's the 'right thing'. Without actually saying it, Jensen is acknowledging Daryl's relationship with Euphie as a marriage of sorts. I imagine it is not easy for him, for marriage is sacred and vows should be taken before God. But Jensen is showing Daryl respect. Perhaps he might even have defended Daryl's life choice to be with the Aboriginal people on the Track if anyone tried to belittle him in Jensen's hearing.

It seems natural to measure the two men against each other. There are parallels in their lives. Both are the same age; both knew about hard work and defined themselves by their work. Both dedicated the prime of their lives to the same Aboriginal people. They both knew those people well and loved them: Jensen loved being around them, appreciated their humour, warmth and generosity; Daryl loved who they were, their values, their way of life, and he loved what they had to teach him. Yet neither man ever met.

Jensen wrote:

> On one occasion someone asked me to take them up to his [Daryl's] place, and as soon as he saw me, he retreated inside quickly and didn't even come to see what we were there about.[19]

Daryl, who at that moment in his life was facing ill-treatment and disrespect from local clients who had always before dealt with his brother and were not happy to have to deal with the fellow who had Aboriginal children, was clearly afraid of Alwyn Jensen. He was not to know and would never know that Jensen and he were essentially on the same side when it came to Aboriginal people. Jensen came to them in good faith and through his dealings with them met Doug Nicholls and then Stan Davey of the Victorian Aboriginal Advancement League. He took on the politics of the League and realised that he had to do something to protect the people he was learning to love from the Aborigines Welfare Board. He knew the Board would inevitably move them from the Track and so he cooperated with the Housing Commissioner Harry Davey to find housing for them that seemed to be in keeping with his philosophy. He thought he could control the Board that way, but the Board was part of the state bureaucracy and rolled on ruthlessly.

When everything was finally finished, when the Aboriginal people had been dispersed and neither man was connected with them as they had been, Jensen could go on with his other life. He had his farm, his wife, his children and his church. Daryl Tonkin had nothing.

ENDNOTES

[1] B357/0 Box 5; Office of Chief Secretary of Vic, Hon, Rylah, Press Statement 27 August 1962.

[2] B357/0 Box 5. Press Statement 27 August 1962.

[3] B357/0 Box 5: Drouin 'camp' Princes Highway, Letter from P. E. Felton to M C Taylor, 11 May 1962.

[4] Perks and Thomson (1998 p. ix).

[5] Phrase used by W. E. H. Stanner in his Boyer Lectures (Stanner 1968).

[6] See Bain Attwood's discussion in *The making of the Aborigines* (Attwood 1989, p. 136).

[7] Interview with Dot Mullett, Warragul, 20 April 2004.

[8] Mr Jensen would later become involved in evangelistic tent crusades that emerged – or were revived – with the Australian tour of Billy Graham in the late sixties.

[9] Interview with Flo Cowden White, Warragul, 22 April 2004. All direct quotes from Flo White in this chapter are from this interview unless specifically identified as coming from other sources.

[10] Interview with Alwyn Jensen, Neerim South, 8 April 2004. All direct quotes from Mr Jensen in this chapter are from this interview unless specifically identified as coming from other sources.

[11] Wurm (1963, p. 2).

[12] Alwyn Jensen, *Report to NBAAL AGM 1967* from the papers of Hector Cowden.

[13] Bain Attwood (2003, p. xiii) make similar comments.

[14] Letter from Alwyn Jensen to Carolyn Landon, 28 February 2006.

[15] Mullett interview.

[16] Letter from Alwyn Jensen to Carolyn Landon, 28 February 2006.

[17] B357/0 Box 5: Drouin 'camp' Prices Highway 1958–64, Report by A. Jensen to P. Felton, 19 August 1959.

[18] B357/0 Box 5, Report by A. Jensen to P. Felton; and letter from A. Jensen to J. H. Davey (Board Housing Member), 20 May 1959.

[19] Letter from Alwyn Jensen to Carolyn Landon, 28 February 2006.

REFERENCES

Attwood, Bain. 1989. *The making of the Aborigines*. Sydney: Allen & Unwin.
Attwood, Bain. 2003. *Rights for Aborigines*. Sydney: Allen & Unwin.
Perks, R.; Thomson, A. 1998. 'Introduction'. In *The oral history reader*. London: Routledge.
Stanner, W. E. H. 1968. *After the Dreaming*. Sydney: ABC Books.
Wurm, S. A. 1963. *Some remarks on the role of language in the assimilation of Australian Aborigines*. Canberra: Linguistic Circle of Canberra Publications.

Cite this chapter as: Landon, Carolyn. 2006. 'Mr Jensen's story'. In *Jackson's Track revisited: History, remembrance and reconciliation*. Melbourne: Monash University ePress. pp. 5.1–5.18. DOI: 10.2104/jtr06005.

CHAPTER 6

THE STORY THE NEWSPAPERS TELL

Carolyn Landon

Attitudes in the local and state-wide newspapers, reflecting those found in the Archive, construct an idea of Aboriginality that proves difficult to shake. Scandalous reports about goings on amongst newly 'assimilated' neighbours in the area represent Aboriginal people as children or animals, a primitive race, stone-age people, static, unchanging and dying out. Paradoxically, however, these media reports tend to express a desire to welcome Aboriginal people into 'civilised' settler society, to offer them civil rights, and give them opportunities to change their ways. This chapter paints a picture of failure of policy, and attempts to demonstrate what went wrong and why.

In the introduction to her book *Untold stories*, Jan Critchett admits to being 'impressed and then appalled at the quantity and detail of the information [about Aborigines] that survived in official records'.[1] I too am amazed and appalled at the amount of material there is available in the Archive about the people who had lived at the Track. Ian McFarlane from the Public Records Office of Victoria writes:

> Aboriginal people... had long been under the microscope. Their activities and 'morality' were constantly monitored and analysed... Commentaries about individual Aboriginals disregarded all principles of privacy. [That] some documents read like a script for a modern 'soap opera' is revealing.[2]

Hector Cowden's daughter, Flo, said that her father was disgusted with the Aborigines Welfare Board because the officers who dealt most closely with the Aboriginal people – Regional Commissioner of Housing H. Davey and Regional Director P. Felton – dehumanised them with labels and categories and with the details they reported about them in their official capacities. It is true that I feel almost voyeuristic looking at lists of people I know, finding details about their lives to which I should never be party. And it is true that while I am uncomfortable reading these lists, I have the distinct impression that nowhere am I finding any truth about the people on them. There is no true indication of their characters, their opinions, their values, their needs, their culture. It is impossible to hear their voices. Critchett says, 'Perhaps it was my new preoccupation with individuals that opened my eyes'.[3] It is my new preoccupation with one of these individuals in particular that has opened mine.

In one list I find a reference to Jimmy Bond and in an instant Pauline, who has been absent during my talk with Mr Jensen, is back with me, looking over my shoulder, waiting to see my reaction. I know Jimmy Bond. He, along with Dave Moore, was Daryl Tonkin's best friend on the Track. While Dave was a teacher, storyteller and hunter in the community, Jimmy became a skilled worker. Daryl trusted him to be in charge of the fence posts and eventually had him working on the saws at the mill. Jimmy was a loyal friend to Daryl, 'a man I could count on', he said.[4] When recounting how Jimmy was killed in a hit-and-run incident on the highway, Daryl described exactly what kind of a man Jimmy Bond was:

> He was one of the old breed of blackfella. It's hard to explain just what the qualities were that these old fellas had, but there's no match for them today. You never saw such workers as the old ones. Gee, they were skilful people and they had the heart to tackle any job... And they looked like quality. I don't know what it was that let you identify the quality in them, maybe they walked in a graceful, silent sort of way with their heads up noticing everything around them... I don't know, there was something about Jimmy that was hard to explain – a kind of spirit.[5]

In a 1958 report to the Chief Secretary's Department, Jimmy Bond is listed as a 'hanger-on' at the shack of Sid Austin.[6] Other names the Board gives to people not, according to the Board, in the right place at the right time, are: *blow-ins, lay-abouts, wanderers*.[7] Of course, Jimmy wasn't a hanger-on. Apart from being a skilled worker, he was the self-appointed protector of the community at the Track. After everyone was dispersed, he made the rounds, on foot or hitchhiking, from Neerim South to Rokeby to the highway camp at Drouin back to the Track – a round trip of about thirty-five kilometres – to keep track of everyone and keep people in touch with one another. Everyone trusted and relied on Jimmy Bond, yet the only reference to him in the Archives is that he was a 'hanger-on'.

In his report to the Chief Secretary, the Aborigines Welfare Officer M. C. Taylor talked of speaking with 'Mrs Dave Mullett'.[8] When I read that name I am on the alert. I know this woman to be Euphemia Hood, Daryl's wife and Pauline's mother, and I know that by 1958 she had not been anywhere near Dave Mullett for twelve years. I also know that she did not think of herself as Mullett's wife, and nor did anybody else besides Mr Taylor. I wonder how he knew her name was Mrs Dave Mullett. Did Euphie tell him? If so, why? Was she afraid of the authorities and so reverted to her official Lake Tyers name? Or was it a clever feint on her part to keep him ignorant of her current life, to tell him only what she wanted him to hear and no more? What does Pauline think? Later, when I show her Taylor's comments, she tells me that her Mum would have given her official married name because she thought her father might land in gaol if it were known he was the father of her children: "After all, Aunty Joycie's man was thrown in Pentridge for the same thing!" said Pauline.[9]

In his report Mr Taylor detailed how many children Euphie had. He also stated – in spite of what he knew (that 'Mrs Mullett' was living with 'a Mr Tonkin', whom he described as White and the father of some of Euphie's children) or because of what Euphie told him – where he believed Dave Mullett to be. The shape and wording of this report seems to me to include a snide accusation of 'miscegenation and 'promiscuity'[10] on the part of Taylor who knew, as Euphie and Daryl seemed not to, that it was no longer considered an offence for a White person to 'consort' with an Aboriginal person. The law had changed with the formation of the Welfare Board and as a response to McLean's report, but the accusation of 'miscegenation and sexual promiscuity' prevailed.

The Archives, more than anything, show the workings of the bureaucracy and the preoccupations and attitudes of the bureaucrats. In the documents relating to Aboriginal housing in Drouin from 1958 to the late 1960s, an incredible story unfolds of a struggle between the League led by Jensen, the Board led by Felton and Harry Davey, and the Buln Buln Shire Council influenced, it seems, by the overt racism of Gus Stoll. As soon as the Board discovered the existence of the group at the Track, a fight for control of lives ensued. As we have seen, Jensen wanted to convert Aborigines but in doing God's work he became concerned with their physical well-being. He felt the families at the Track were in dire need of new housing, and so he turned to the Board for help in financing such a project. He knew that the Board would not agree to improving conditions at the Track. He also knew that the Board was adamant about moving people into towns. Because he had misgivings about the Board's plan, he went looking for suitable spots to shift families to, with the aim of improving their lives and at the same time maintaining for them the safety of distance from interfering on-lookers. "Now, I knew they had to have decent homes," he said, "but I thought it was a crying shame to put them into a nice home alongside people who didn't understand."[11]

He found two houses, one in Neerim South for the Austin family, Jensen's most responsive recruits to God's message, and another in Rokeby for another family he hadn't yet decided on. The Austins were cousins of the Hoods and constant companions of the

Mullett-Tonkin brood so their shift away from the Track was keenly felt by Daryl, to say nothing of all of his children and Stewart and Dora Hood. Unlike Cowden, it appears that Jensen did not have a sense of this social context or feel that the Austins were an integral part of a functioning community. In his interview, he seems pleased with himself at finding what he considered appropriate housing and at a good price of £100 for house and land. "Actually, I bought two of the houses, down here in Rokeby, two railway houses," he says. "I bought them and Harry Davey said to me 'Look, seeing you're going to help, if you see any houses, let us know and we'll have a look at them.' I said, 'Right. There's two already available.' Because I had it in mind... I would have paid for it myself if I could have afforded it."[12] He pressured the Board to pay for the houses. This activity makes Jensen look more like a collaborator than a controller of the Board. He would be dismayed to realise that is how he comes across in the record. Certainly Daryl thought he was a collaborator and, until I met Jensen, I thought so too. I wonder what the Aboriginal people thought?

At around the time Jensen located the railway houses, Mrs Rosamond Comber, a friend of Mrs Buchanan, offered a five-acre paddock near Drouin to the Board for lease at one shilling per annum. Jensen got busy finding a 'bungalow in Catani' for £50 to move to Comber's land and the League men got together to 'make habitable' a small two-room cottage that came with the lease.[13] These dwellings were meant for Stewart and Dora Hood and soon afterwards the Rose family, who wouldn't stay at the Track if their Ma and Pop (Dora and Stewart Hood) were taken away. Meanwhile Bill and Pen Buchanan sold a block of land on Wood Street in Drouin to the Board for £200 where 'the Board wishes to have a small house built for an aboriginal family of two adults and seven small children now living in a humpy on Jackson's Track... The Board's objective is to bring them nearer to possible venues of employment and medical attention.'[14] There is no mention of who this family was and why they needed medical attention. Housing Commissioner J. H. Davey, not to be confused with Stan Davey from the League, wrote to Jensen (not the Buchanans) that he would see if the Housing Commission would build a house on the land. It turned out that Parliament had to amend the Board's legislative powers to enable the Housing Commission to build. Finally, the 'State CWA [Country Women's Association] Thanksgiving Fund amounting to 1500 pounds was given to this project'[15] and the house was built and ready for occupancy in August 1960, almost two years after it was needed.

All this activity seems productive and could be called good works, except that there is no mention whatsoever of any sort of consultation process with the Aboriginal people themselves. In fact, there is hardly any mention at all of the individuals who would be most affected. I know from Daryl's memoir that it upset the whole community at the Track, not least Daryl Tonkin himself. I wonder what Jensen told them: that he was moving them in the name of God or in the name of the Board or in the name of the League? Did the Aboriginal people ask Jensen for help? Did he have discussions about the moves with Stewart Hood? Did Hood, who was an Elder and the leader at the camp, advise Jensen on who to move and where to move them? There is nothing in the Archives, nothing in the local papers. When I ask Jensen if the Aboriginal people asked him to find houses for them he says "No, well, they didn't ask as such because that's not their nature, but, no, I can't remember they asked me to get them a home. But it was my idea to get them a house not totally isolated..."[16]

I wonder what Jensen means about their *nature*. And I wonder what other words such as *humpy* and *hanger-on* indicate about who these people think *Aborigines/Aboriginal people* are. Clearly they had assumptions about what made their charges – why did they see them as *charges*? – different from themselves. I see a variety of attitudes being expressed time and time again that I would have thought had been erased by the 1960s. These attitudes, found in the public record in the Archive, construct an idea of Aboriginality that is very hard to shake. Beckett explains of the idea of Aboriginality that 'there has never been unanimity. Nor has one construction ever been completely erased by its successors – unpopular ideas linger, to reappear at another time, perhaps a different context.'[17] So Jensen can see Aboriginal people as children; Councillor Stoll, as I shall discover, can see them as animals; and all can see them as a primitive race, stone-age people, static, unchanging and dying out. At the same time, they want to welcome them into the civilised settler society, offer them civil rights, and give them opportunities to change their ways.

As soon as the people are moved into town things begin to go wrong. *The Warragul Gazette* reports that when residents heard the Wood Street property was for the express purpose of housing Aborigines, they got up a petition protesting that land values would go down and handed it to the Shire Council. Later, when the Board asked the Council to reduce rates for their housing, Councillor Stoll said 'If the request were acceded to the Aborigines would be able to drink more and lay about drunk in parks'.[18] At Comber's five-acre paddock – the camp on the highway – it takes more than a year to complete a kitchen for the Rose family, who are living in the bungalow, and to get the stove working in the Hood's kitchen (meanwhile they are cooking outside on an open fire). There is no water and only one 'bush dunny', which Jensen calls a toilet. "Proper toilets", but which he quickly amends to "a dunny, not like we have",[19] had been erected for four adults and seven children.

Flo White remembers that the camp on the highway "wasn't a place where you played. It was a very exposed cold place, facing west and open to the wind... very different environment to the Track."[20] She recalls her father being dismayed at the conditions at the camp for the Aboriginal people who moved there. "That was Dad's main beef," she said, "that there had been a plan to move these people... but the move had not been thought that well through and the place was not ready for the number of people or for their needs."[21]

Picture of 'the camp' from *The Gippsland Independent,* 19 September 1963.
(Reproduced courtesy of the Warragul Historical Society)

Finally, the whole project of improving conditions became a disaster in the eyes of the non-Aboriginals whose vision it had been for Aboriginal people to eventually join the community as good, hard working, religious citizens. It is apparent that Jensen and Cowden blamed the Board for interfering and telling people what to do. The Board made decisions about who would live in which houses, after Jensen had moved the Austins, the Hoods and Roses without 'proper' procedure. When Jensen and Buchanan made suggestions about who deserved to find a good house, the Board rejected their advice with decisions that seem arbitrary.

"Oh, yes," laughed Jensen, "the Board had a lot less respect for them [Aboriginal people] than the League did. The Board was only implementing the policies of the Government."[22]

Control of the whole situation was eventually up for grabs, for it turned out that the Aboriginal people for whom everything was being done were not interested in changing their way of living. The Board began to complain that they couldn't keep people in the houses they were put in. Field Officers couldn't keep track of who was where and seemed to spend much of their time counting people. They became exasperated at the number of people living in particular houses. At one point there were as many as twenty-three people staying at the Wood Street residence. The Austin house was always full. Police were called to move on boyfriends, 'hangers-on', 'family'. Jensen reports to Harry Davey that 'Drunkenness is rife at the moment [at the Camp on the highway] with passing aborigines calling in and bringing liquor'.[23] Later, Davey notes to Felton:

> For information and necessary action: visited camp... noticed a tent well in the background carefully concealed in the bush; understand it is occupied by a Dowell [this is actually Dow, Aunty Joycie's white husband with whom she has already had nine children and will go on to have nine more; it is the same man who was gaoled for consorting with Aunty Joycie, according to Pauline] a white man with an aboriginal wife and nine children. Mrs Jensen told me the conditions there are extremely squalid – youngsters in poor condition with sores, etc.[24]

It wasn't until 1964 that the Board finally took the action Davey was looking for, but this was after scandalous reports about goings on at the Camp had begun circulating in the towns, the local media, and finally the statewide newspaper *The Age*. The League members seemed to concede defeat. It turned out that the Aborigines were intractable. All except Ma Hood had turned away from Jensen's church. His idea of transitional housing was not working since they could not control those very same characteristics of 'the Aboriginal' that McLean had warned of in his report: living for the present with 'lack of thought for tomorrow', strong family ties, the 'habit' of sharing 'which is deeply rooted among them'.[25] In defeat, the League appealed to the Council to condemn the very camp they had so hopefully set up for the Aborigines (in order to get the Board to take action and find proper new houses in the town). They also asked the Council to move on or gaol whomever else was 'squatting' there. At a meeting in June 1963, the Council moved to cancel the lease at the camp. In support of this motion the Shire Health Inspector said, 'The aboriginal settlement [i.e., the 'camp'] is like a boil. Others move in on the people who were there and they move off. It is not a condition that should exist in this municipality'. Councillor Stoll argued against the request. 'These people know their way of life', he said, 'and why should the Council make any decision that they were not happy? Treat these people as if they were one of us'.[26] At first it is hard to know what Stoll means here; it seems a sympathetic statement, but that is not in the man's character; elsewhere there is angry correspondence to the paper about him refusing to let Aboriginal people live anywhere near him. It seems he sees these people as animals and is saying they are probably happy living like animals.

Headlines from the local papers
(Papers held by the Warragul Historical Society)

The Council passed the motion despite Councillor Stoll's protests. They called for and heard more reports about the possible transmission of disease – specifically infective hepatitis (which had been found locally on some farms but never at the 'Camp') – from the Health Inspector, about fire danger from the Fire Officer, about condemned housing from the Housing Inspector. The Council served writs of eviction on the Hoods and Roses without offering them alternative housing. This incensed Jensen, who informed Davey, and the writs never took effect. The Council went over everyone's heads and wrote to the Premier, Henry Bolte, sending a copy of the letter to the Board. This sent the Board into a panic and resulted in an angry letter from The Honourable E. R. Meagher, Chairman of the Board. By this time most of the Neerim League members seemed to have run for cover for they can no longer be found in the Record. Animated debate at Council meetings included talk of Aborigines living in filth, of 'foul conditions not fit for human habitation', accusations of irresponsibility, and finally absolute condemnation of the whole enterprise.[27]

When I read through all the documents and see this story build before my eyes, characters emerge in my imagination. Mr Jensen's enthusiasm and energy, as well as his disappointment and even embarrassment as things go wrong, are abundantly clear in these papers. Felton's assumption of superiority and sense of his own power comes through in his decrees to Harry Davey about who should live where and when. Davey is a practical man working at the coal-face and reporting dutifully to his bosses; Jensen tells me that he and Harry Davey had great battles, that Davey wouldn't 'bend'. The Honourable Meagher remains a shadow, deigning to come down from his tower only once in a while. The Shire Councillors are rural council stereotypes, conservative and complacent men who base their decisions mostly on local knowledge and practical common sense, except for Gus Stoll who is outspoken, racist and angry.

As for the Aboriginal characters at the centre of it all, I can get no picture of them. They seem to be stock characters, constructed for convenience. They are merely named – or if they are not named, they are given tags such as *hanger-on* – as if the names are labels on cardboard cut outs. The labelling and systematic categorisation of people demonstrates a profound lack of respect; it erases human dignity. If you steal people's humanity it is easy to conclude that they have no culture, no history, no spiritual belief, no morality, no law. Assimilation seems like a good solution for a people who are left voiceless, completely silent. Yet the officals on the Board or in the Buln Buln Shire found out they were not so easy to assimilate.

This is a story of concerned people, overbearing in their enthusiasm, trying to control, help, erase or convert another people whom they seemed to completely misunderstand. The members of the Welfare Board, who mismanaged this debacle with the unwitting help of honest, but possibly misguided, local people, thought that by adopting the policy

"How do we stop them living there"

Cr. Kraft Asks a Most Important Question

...s in a quandary as to how to get ...uin West aborigine camp, who had before them a further con-...)fficer of Health, Dr. E. J. C. ...rought to the attention of the ...is published in full on page 2

...re alternative accommodation ...p? Apparently the board has ...; no intention of shifting these

"Cattle are cared for but Aborigines are not"

— CR. W. J. BLOYE

Following upon the reading of a scathing report by the Medical Officer (Dr. E. J. C. Hamp), on the unsavoury conditions obtaining at an aborigines' settlement in the Buln Buln Shire, and a further report in similar vein by the Health Inspector (Mr. W. C. Walker), council is obviously very disturbed.

At last meeting of the council a lengthy debate culminated in a council decision to tell the Aborigines Welfare Board that for health reasons the settlement was to be closed down and that the board would have to find suitable alternative housing for these people outside the town boundaries.

Councillors were shocked at the filthy and appalling conditions under which the aborigines were living as described in the reports. They treated full discussion of the situation as an urgent measure.

Cr. Bloye : "I feel very strongly about this. I think anything that is done should be done from the point of giving them better conditions.

"This is a reproach on all of us to shut our eyes to the fact that fellow humans beings are allowed to live under such conditions. They are not allowed to do much for themselves and it is the responsibility of this community to do something for them.

"What are we going to do? That is the challenge to all of us."

The President (Cr. R. Henry) : "Should we bring it before the proper authorities?"

Cr. Bloye : "Before closing down this settlement we should provide better accommodation.

Cr. C. M. Stoll : "I do not think that this should have to be borne by this council. Where is the £100,000 allocated for the aborigines' welfare? Why should this council have to

pressure on the Aborigine Welfare Board to do something."

Cr. Bloye : "Could Cr. Price add to his motion that this council considers the matter urgent due to the unsanitary conditon?"

Cr. Price : "If we close it within 30 days the board has got to do something."

Cr. Bloye : "I will move an amendment that alternative accommodation must be provided. They are human beings."

Cr. Price : "They would be better on the road."

Voices : "No."

Cr. Bloye : "I am very concerned from the humanitarian point of view, and anything we do should be on behalf of the poor people out there.

"If you turn cattle out they go to the pound - they are fed and looked after. These people are not.

"I think pressure should be brought on to the board to provide alternative accommodation. What they have now is some shelter at least."

do something about it? Why cannot they set up a type of house outside the town?

"The aborigine will tell you himself that he does not want to live in the main street. I think we should press the Government to make this money available to build houses on the outskirts of the town and not built up areas."

Cr. M. C. Price moved that council notify the Aborigine Welfare Board that conditions at the settlement are not up to medical health standards and if nothing is done within 30 days council will have no option but to close it."

Cr. Stoll : "Why do not people who own the land out there cancel the lease?"

VERY URGENT

Cr. Price : "What I have heard here today is very urgent. In 60 days we will

"THEY WILL DIE"

Cr. Saunders : "The motion is more strong than the amendment. That is why I am against the amendment."

Both Crs. Stoll & Bertram supported the ammendment.

Cr. N. E. Nicholson: "You have only to read the report. We do employ a Health Inspector and we

Queen could do no wrong. A spanner had been thrown into the works.

"Board's Responsibility"

Lease of the camp area to the board at 1/- a year had been extended for another twelve months.

Cr. Bloye: "The board would be happy to see the board's responsibility to demolish them."

Cr. M. C. Price: "The only answer is to go to the Premier's level."

On the motion of Cr. Price council revoked a previous resolution which read "that council be assured that alternative accommodation is available for the inhabitants of the

Continued on back page.

Articles from *The Gippsland Independent* —15 August 1963 (front), and 24 September 1963 (back)
(Reproduced courtesy of the Warragul Historical Society)

of assimilation they were generously welcoming the poor and battered native with open arms into a better way of life, a civilised life.

From my point of view in 2004, it occurs to me to ask who should have been doing the welcoming here? The invaders to this land? Or the original inhabitants? It seems to me that when White Australians opened their arms in generous welcome, they had no right to expect Aboriginal people to be grateful. No wonder the Kurnai people of Gippsland seemed uncooperative. They could see that people like Jensen and Aunty Pen were being kind to them, but the idea that they were being welcomed into the whitefellas' way of life would not have made sense to them. They already had a way of life, a way of being, and White Australians knew that. McLean knew it: why didn't he take advantage of what he knew instead of trying to wean the Aboriginal people away from their way of life to fit White Australian constructions of who they were? Why did the Board set itself up in conflict with the League instead of in cooperation with it? Why did it bowl over people like Jensen and Cowden? Why was it so arrogant?

ENDNOTES

[1] Critchett (1999, p. xv).

[2] MacFarlane (1993, p 69).

[3] Critchett (1999, p. xv).

[4] Landon and Tonkin (1999, p. 167).

[5] Landon and Tonkin (1999, p. 245).

[6] B337, Housing – Drouin, Item 7, Report 4 December 1958.

[7] B337, Housing – Drouin, Item 7, Report 4 December 1958, repeated in various reports and letters.

[8] B337, Housing – Drouin, Item 7, Report 4 December 1958.

[9] Interview with Pauline Mullett and Daryl Mobourne, Drouin, 31 May 2004.

[10] McLean Inquiry, Item, 10: McLean, Charles, Report Upon the Operation of the Aborigines Act 1928 and the Regulations and Order made Thereunder, Melbourne, 1957, B408. p. 6.

[11] Interview with Alwyn and Hilda Jensen, Neerim South, 8 April 2004.

[12] Jensen interview.

[13] B357 Box 5: Drouin Lease. Comber's Land. Princes Highwqay, Drouin East. Report from Chief Secretary's Department signed by P.E. Felton, Regional Supervisor of Aborigines Welfare 29 July 1958.

[14] B357/0 'Drouin Wood Street Purchase', Letter, 6 August 1958.

15   *Warragul Gazette*, 'New Home for Aborigines', 2August 1960.

16   Jensen interview.

17   Beckett (1988, p. 196.)

18   B336 Box 3 'Drouin and District Rates. Districts – Gippsland 1959-26,' extract Warragul Gazette, December 1960.

19   Jensen interview.

20   Interview with Flo Cowden White, Warragul, 22 April 2004.

21   White interview.

22   Jensen interview.

23   B357/0 Box 5 Drouin Camp Princes Highway 1958-64, League Annual Report Concerning Camp, 25 June 1959.

24   B357/0 Box 5, League Annual Report Concerning Camp. Note, Davey to Felton, 23 December 1959.

25   McLean report.

26   *Gippsland Independent*, 'Aboriginal Settlement Danger to Health,' 20 June 1963, p. 4.

27   *The Age*, 21 April 1964, p. 3; *The Gippsland Independent*, 19 September 1963, p. 1.

REFERENCES

Beckett, Jeremy. 1988. *The past in the present; The present in the past: Constructing a national Aboriginality*. Canberra: Aboriginal Studies Press for the Australian Institute of Aboriginal Studies.

Critchett, Jan. 1999. *Untold stories, memories and lives of Victorian Kooris*. Melbourne: Melbourne University Press.

Landon, Carolyn; Tonkin, Daryl. 1999. *Jackson's Track: Memoir of a Dreamtime place*. Melbourne: Penguin.

MacFarlane, Ian. 1993. 'Glimpses from the past'. In *My heart is breaking: A joint guide to the records about Aboriginal people in the Public Records Office of Victoria and the Australian Archives, Victorian Regional Office*. Canberra: Australian Government Publishing Service.

Cite this chapter as: Landon, Carolyn. 2006. 'The story the newspapers tell'. In *Jackson's Track revisited: History, remembrance and reconciliation*. Melbourne: Monash University ePress. pp. 6.1–6.12. DOI: 10.2104/jtr06006.

CHAPTER 7

AUNTY GINA'S STORY

Carolyn Landon

"Why don't they ever talk to us?" asks Pauline Mullett, daughter of Daryl Tonkin, who initiated the telling of the Jackson's Track story by asking her father to break his silence. In this chapter, the historian speaks with Aunty Gina Rose, the Elder of the local Kurnai people. After an initial discussion of protocols and hierarchical arrangements that White Australians must try to understand and honour, Aunty Gina tells her story. Her narrative is supported by the testimony of other Kurnai people who lived and grew up on Jackson's Track and remember the move into town that so devastated Daryl Tonkin. The way the Kurnai people see themselves has escaped the constructions White Australians have placed upon them ever since invasion.

Six years ago, not many months after *Jackson's Track* was published, Pauline and I gave an Australia Day speech to the people of Drouin, the seat of the old Buln Buln Shire. The Shire had no idea that inviting Pauline to speak at such an event would cause her pain but, in spite of her strong political objection to attending a celebration of what to her was an invasion, she decided the book had given her a right to tell the people of Drouin who she was. She had never spoken to a large group of White people before, certainly not in the community where she had grown up. After I introduced her, she stood trembling with nerves before an audience filled with many people she knew: on the one hand school teachers who had punished her, school mates who had bullied her, police who had harassed her; on the other hand team mates who had helped her become a badminton champion, colleagues who had encouraged her, and others who had come to know of and respect her through her father's book. She spoke clearly to them all:

> I wonder if you realise that the Aboriginal people who have always lived in Gippsland are called Kurnai? We have always been here; we never left; we never returned; we have been here forever. I am proud to say I am Kurnai.
>
> I wonder if you know that on the Lake Tyers Mission Station we were not allowed to speak our language or perform our rituals or educate our children in our traditions? I wonder if you know that our implements, paintings, sacred symbols – our past – were locked up in the museum and kept away from us?

But now we have the key to unlock our memories. It is like a beginning for us in that we are returning to our most important duty and that is the care of our land and our culture. You may know that the land is so integrated with the culture that you cannot separate them.

It may seem as if the culture is returning to us, when actually it has never been lost, only hidden. The elders have made it their duty to guard our culture, like a hidden treasure, passing it down to a chosen few who would keep the stories. The storytellers were invested by the elders with our ancient memories and so they have never been lost.

Now we are all learning our stories. We are remembering how important they are, and we are confident enough to let you hear some of them.[1]

I didn't know then, as I listened to Pauline speak, that all she said was true. In fact I imagined that much of it was symbolic – until Pauline arranged for me to interview her Aunty Gina Rose.

Regina Hood Rose is the most important person in her group. She is the Elder, the head of the family. There are other elders in the tribe who are members of other branches of the family and she cannot do anything without consulting them and reaching consensus. However, the Native Title Claim for Kurnai Land, which covers most of Gippsland, is being made in Aunty Gina's name and everyone in the group defers to her. She is Pauline's aunt, Euphemia's sister; she is the wife of Roy Rose and mother of Lionel. Roy Rose was from Warnambool – Framlingham – where Aunty Gina's grandfather, Collin Hood, came from. Collin Hood was a Djab Wurrung man born in 1836. He left his country for Gippsland, of his own accord after certain tragedies and disappointments in the 1890s.[2] After settling at Ramahyuck Mission Station, he married Helen, daughter of Kitty Perry Johnson. Kitty was a Kurnai woman of the Brabralung Clan whose country is 'four days walk north of the ancient common corroboree site near Swan Reach on Lake King'.[3] She was one of the old people who knew tribal law in that she walked the land her ancestors had walked for forty-thousand years or more. From Kitty the line goes directly through to Pauline – from her mother Euphemia and her Aunty Gina.[4] When I think of this lineage and the importance of Aunty Gina's role among the Kurnai, I wonder how those men of the assimilation era with their assumption of racial superiority could have looked her in the eye. One would think that this proud and dignified woman

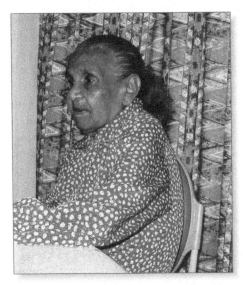

Aunty Gina
Photo by the author

would have dashed to rubble any skerrick of superiority lurking in their poor whitefella frames.

Aunty Gina was born at Lake Tyers, lived with her mother and sister Euphemia near Dimboola for some time, then began to 'follow the peas' – seasonal vegetable picking work – after her mother returned to Gippsland. She settled at Jackson's Track with her mother and father in the late 1940s and lived there as an unmarried young woman under the protection of her parents before she met and married Roy Rose.

I have learned by listening and watching that it is correct etiquette to introduce Aboriginal people this way, by identifying them through family and country. It is satisfying to read Diane Barwick's explanation of this practice in her review of Philip Pepper's autobiography:

> Victorian Aborigines of Pepper's generation were primarily defined by place of origin and family membership. To 'place' a new acquaintance they asked where he came from and which family he belonged to, not what jobs he did or what opinions he held.[5]

If I am to speak freely with Pauline's family, I need to know how to behave and they need to know who I am. I am a *gubbah* or *wadjiman* both of which mean whitefella. The words are sometimes pejorative depending on when they are used and who might say them, but usually they are just generic. In this company, I am a *whitefella* and they are *blackfellas*,[6] although outside the relaxed atmosphere of family they are Kurnai. Pauline seems to have created a place of trust for me here, primarily by allowing me to work with her father, and everyone in the family knows about the book and refers to it when they speak to me. It seems to demonstrate to them my interest in them, my willingness to learn, as well as my respect and compassion. I hope the atmosphere of trust will continue even if I still do not understand everything. Pauline is confident I do not have a hidden agenda: I do not want to convert anyone; I do not want to change anyone's life; I do not want to exploit anyone; I am not judgemental. However, it takes frequent expressions of reassurance throughout my time with Pauline's family to maintain their trust in me. Certainly, judging from the history I have so far uncovered, they have a right to wonder at my motives, to be doubtful of my intention to treat their stories with respect. They know what I am not entirely aware of yet: that my whitefella construction of their character and place in history may cloud my ability to see them for who they are.

Of course, I have been in Aunty Gina's company several times before, but this is the first time I have ever tried to speak to her formally while recording her voice and taking notes. I am concerned that I am about to bring up painful events for her to remember and wonder how forthcoming she will be. I have met other grey-haired Aboriginal people who will not speak about times past for it is too painful; I know that the testimonies collected by the Koori Heritage Trust in Melbourne are tightly guarded to maintain confidentiality, for many stories are indictments of people still living. I wonder if Aunty Gina will be guarded and wary; I wonder if she will censor herself as she constructs her narrative to protect her family and to keep me happy. After all, I have already seen in the lists of Board records how her people allowed bureaucrats to misconstrue their identities and motives. Pauline has told me she will be on the lookout for such feints coming from her Aunty.

Foolishly, I think I know what Aunty Gina is going to tell me. From reading the records, listening to the narratives of Jensen and Flo White, and working intensively with Daryl Tonkin on his memoir, I have formed a strong opinion about what has happened in the past and how it has affected the Aboriginal people. I assume that they felt degraded by the scandal that seemed to encompass their very existence when they lived on Comber's five acres out on the highway near the racetrack, the five acres that the Board called 'the Camp' and the League called 'the Settlement'. I assume that they still have strong feelings of sadness and anger as a result of the insults directed at them in the public arena and the eventual breaking up of the community that lived at the Camp and on the Track. I believe that they have been in a state of shock for the last forty years for that is the state in which I found Daryl Tonkin when I began working with him, and certainly his memoir bears the scars of grief, regret and bitterness.

As it turns out, I couldn't have been more wrong.

When I talk with her, we are sitting in Aunty Gina's house in Drouin. It is a newish place and seems large and rambling. I think there are lots of rooms off the lounge room with people in them who come and go. That is one thing about Aboriginal houses: they are fully occupied all of the time.[7] A large television is on in the lounge room and two young women with their boisterous children are watching it now and again. Pauline, Aunty Gina and I are sitting at a table near the kitchen. I have brought some cake and the children keep running up to grab pieces of it, fighting over it. I have all these sounds on audio tape: not only Aunty Gina's voice, but also the mothers scolding the kids and doors opening and shutting in the background. Aunty Gina sits entirely composed next to me at the table and ignores it all, except when one of the kids jostles her – then she raises her voice at the mothers to control the children. She remains focused on her narrative throughout. She answers my questions thoroughly and deliberately.

First I ask her what it was like living at Jackson's Track:

> Well, it was really good being out there and being out in the bush life, like the old people used to do, I mean. We had a bark hut. It had a bark roof and a tent.

> I think I was around sixteen then. We were in Dimboola and then we went to Bunyip picking beans and peas and then from there to the Track. That's when Dad got us in there and we lived there ever since. There was plenty of work there for the men. Yeah. They were all getting paid. They were all getting wages...

> We were all happy. There was just me and Euphie – the two sisters – and then there was me brother and me Mum and Dad, our cousins, the Austins. We all lived in the same area. We were up one end of Jackson's Track and they were sort of down near Wattle Creek... That's where the Austins lived down where all those fruit trees were and we were in the middle of Jackson's Track just before McDonalds Road. You know where that next bit goes straight? We were living

back in the bush there. That's where we had those three huts. Hmmm. Yeah that's right. And it was a good life there... My parents were there and Euphie... I wasn't married then. I didn't get married until I met Roy. He was out there. They were all out there at the time: Austins, Roses, Bloomfields – Freddy Bloomfield. They were all working. They were all cutting wood. [Freddy] lived with Aunty Vera Rose and her husband, Johnny, was there... And then there was Lionel and Norma and their son, Steven, and their daughter.[8]

This is the kind of answer I have expected and most of the information she includes is also part of Daryl's story. I then ask her how she came to know the White people Daryl Tonkin called the 'do-gooders' and what kind of a relationship she had with them, but before she gives a direct answer to the question she tells me about how many whitefellas she has known, who she has worked for in her life and how she has been friends with many White people. I wonder if she is trying to make me feel relaxed in her company, but it seems her real motive is to let me know that she knows whitefellas and, in her opinion, they have no control over her. Once that is established she answers my question:

I sort of got to know [the Christians] through Mrs Buchanan. It started when she used to come out to the Track, you know, to bring stuff out to us like clothes. Yeah, she was my friend. I had a lot of time for her... Yeah, I trusted the Buchanans. I trusted the Jensens, too. You know I met them. We thought they were very kind doing what they were doing for us... They used to come down and visit us at the Track... They used to hold... well, we called them meetings in those days, out at the highway. Mr Jensen used to hold them.

I am impressed with Aunty Gina's tone here. There is no wavering or misgiving when she talks of these people. She says she happily accepted their help because to her it was a practical matter of sharing rather than charity. She seems to have no sense that there was any motive or hidden agenda in the actions of the do-gooders. She completely overlooks that they might have assumed superiority over her. In other words, it seems that she accepted their friendship at face value and accepted their help 'in the accustomed manner'[9] as has always been done. It has been clear to me for some time that looking after one another in a communal sense is a cultural practice that Pauline and her people

Daryl and two friends building a bark hut
Photo courtesy of Pauline Mullett

readily maintain and continue. Daryl discussed it in his memoir and I have seen Pauline acting upon this duty in many ways.

Aunty Gina admits that she knew the do-gooders were preaching about Jesus and wanted her to believe what they believed, but she was unaware that they wanted to change her or uplift her. When I ask her if she ever converted to Christianity she laughs behind her hand and gives me a coy look. "No," she says.

Pauline, who has joined in the conversation, laughs raucously. Just as Jensen said, I think to myself: Gina's mum, Dora Hood, was the only one he managed to connect with. I ask if the Jensens or Buchanans tried to convince the people living at the Track that it would be a better life living in Drouin:

> No, they never said anything like that to us. You'd have to talk to Mum and Dad [Dora and Stewart Hood] about that, see, 'cause I was only young. Mum and Dad were still with us then, and they could tell us. We all moved together when we left the Track. We [decided to

move away from the Track] because uh, well, there was no work there. Daryl... there was no work. We lived there for so long... I can't recall what year it was, but there was long... other fellas would come off and on, you know. There'd be a gap in work and they'd go then come back when there was work on. But the work ran out. They were only cutting wood for the Drouin factory – Daryl used to supply the factory. There was plenty of timber in those days, plenty of work, but when we decided to move away, the work was finished. We would have stayed on if there'd been work. There was no more wood. So Roy was put off. He had to take it easy because he did have a weak heart. The reason we left was to find work and we wanted to live closer to Drouin so the kids could go to school... No one asked us to move off there. We just moved on our own... Yeah, I was [sorry to move to Drouin away from the Track]. When I first moved to the highway, the kids were having colds all the time. I thought if it was different where we were they wouldn't be getting sick. In those bark huts [on the Track] they were warm. [On the highway] they were getting colds and all the sickness going around... but then when we finally got used to it, it was good for us.

Again I am surprised at the tone of Aunty Gina's story. There is no rancour, no bitterness or sadness, only a bit of regret, and the regret seems to have nothing to do with the do-gooders. It seems that Aunty Gina's world is a practical one filled with essential issues like health, work, food and family. Her speech is full of verbs, which seem to indicate that she is used to actively managing her life in her own way, according to her own customs and beliefs and the needs of her large, extended family.

But the comment she makes about moving off the Track to find work and to enable the kids to go to school, sticks in my mind. It is too close to a letter in the archive from a member of the Welfare Board to the Housing Commission (probably from Mr Felton to Mr Harry Davey) requesting the building of a small house on the Wood Street block sold to the Board by Mrs Buchanan:

> The Board wishes to have a small house built for an aboriginal family of two adults and seven small children now living in a humpy on Jackson's Track. The Breadwinner of this family is able at present to obtain only intermittent employment and is in receipt of social services

[organised for them by Jensen as he related] for the greater part of the year… The Board's objective is to bring them nearer to possible avenues of employment and medical attention.[10]

It seems odd to me to speak of *breadwinners* in an Aboriginal family, as if their social organisation were just like that of White settler Australians, but it seems Aunty Gina is reflecting these attitudes in her narrative. I also remember a quote from Jensen in a news article. Explaining the purpose of the League, he says: 'There are fifteen children in the four families and the League is keen to see them have opportunities for schooling as other children have'.[11] Again, I wonder if Aunty Gina is reflecting whitefella attitudes she heard over and over again in the 1950s and probably still does to this day. Daryl remembered in his memoir that her son Lionel was notorious for wagging school, and Aunty Gina has a giggle about it herself when she begins to tell me how the kids got to school each morning. Did she really care if the kids went to school? Is Aunty Gina's account of moving away from the Track really what she remembers? Or is my doubt here a matter of my giving too much weight to the machinations of the do-gooders and the Board? Do I lack faith in Aunty Gina's ability to think and act autonomously?

It is not long before I am reassured. She looks at me in a kind of embarrassed way and says, "He [Daryl] had a different opinion to me about what happened". When she follows this statement with a short, apologetic laugh, I realise she has been thinking about how I will react when she tells me her version of the story. I understand that she has determined to tell it anyway even if it contradicts Daryl's version – which by now she knows very well, as does all her family – and even if she risks upsetting Pauline as well as me. I appreciate her candour, for it shows she has decided to be straightforward rather than to placate me.

At the same time I feel a jolt of confusion: I have so many doubts. It is as though my thinking has to be wrenched into gear. As I feel myself resist her story, I wonder if I have been sucked into the archival version of events? I wonder if Daryl constructed a similar version to the archives because he was bound by his social and historical context, no matter how much he wanted to reject it? It is difficult enough to recognise a particular mind-set let alone put it aside so we can be open to different kinds of understanding. Aunty Gina's version of events makes me conscious that attitudes I began acquiring the moment I set foot on Australian soil thirty-seven years ago still persist in me, that I may have brought them to this project. As Beckett says, 'unpopular ideas linger…'[12] Perhaps I unconsciously fall back on the very attitudes I was exposed to over and over again in the late 1960s: the idea that Aboriginals are a static people, unchanging, unable to adapt, incapable of co-existence in the modern world, and that therefore they are a dying race. Do I want to see the Aboriginal people as victims to add pathos to my shame at the treatment my race has meted out to them?

Aunty Gina's story shows me that she never considered herself or her people to be wretched, helpless, degenerate or depraved, despite Jensen's ministry. Can I change my mind? Can I take it all in? Aunty Gina seems to realise I am struggling not to resist her story. She tells me why she thinks Daryl told it the way he did and why it was a tragedy for him. "I reckon he would have felt sad [about our move into town] because he missed us all, hey? We were good company for him, you know."

Pauline agrees with her aunty: "Yes, Dad did miss the company. It was the company that blackfellas lived their culture for. I think that's what kept them together."

Neither of these women thinks that my struggle has to do with my idea of who they are. They see the story clearly in terms of human need and response. I try to clear my mind and think the way they do. When Stewart Hood moved away, Daryl would have known he was about to lose everything he loved. The shift of the Hoods and the Roses to Drouin, coming so soon after the shift of the Austin family to Neerim South – all orchestrated by Jensen – was, as we can see in his memoir, momentous for him. His brother had just died and as a consequence some business clients were lost and others felt they could take advantage of Daryl, the shy and awkward whitefella married to a Black woman. With his business in trouble, he had no means of keeping the Hoods and the Roses at Jackson's Track. He told me about a great debt mounting at Pretty's store in Jindivick where he kept a tab running for any of the blackfellas on the Track – all of whom he saw as members of his family – who might be short on money and supplies. He said it had reached £2000 at one point, an enormous amount in the late 1950s, 'but we paid it all off okay'.[13] Aunty Gina remembers, "We used to get credit at the store when we run out of food. You know. And he [Daryl] was there to help us." Daryl's inability to pay his rates for two years (1958 and 1959) before he got back on his feet again is further testament to his lack of liquidity just after Harry died.[14] Unfortunately, this is exactly the time the League, the Welfare and the Christians became most active. Their presence on the property created arguments between Daryl and his old mentor Stewart Hood. Stewy, in deference to his wife Dora, was willing to listen to their talk and considered them to be good people. But Daryl must have known what was coming: the presence of White men on the property, walking amongst the blackfellas, giving them charity and food, must have been like a knife twisting in his heart.

When Daryl came out of his isolation after forty years and began to construct a narrative around these memories, he seems to have compressed what must have been a series of events into one terrible day. For that's how it was to him, one overwhelming event. But it was he who felt the tragedy, not the blackfellas. Most of the other aspects of his version tally with the alternative versions I have heard. For instance, both Jensen and Aunty Gina tell me in their interviews that Jensen did take them all away on the back of a truck, just as Daryl remembers. That truck pulling away from the Track and disappearing down the road must have been a climactic moment for Daryl. It was a moment of righteous goodness for Jensen. For the blackfellas it seemed to be little more than a practical way to get where they were going.

And then there is the bulldozing. It is very hard to get a clear story from Aunty Gina about the destruction of the huts. Yes, she agrees they were bulldozed. No, she can't remember seeing it happen. Yes, it happened very soon after they left. Did it happen on the same day that she left on the truck? Or did it happen long after the blackfellas had gone, in 1962 when Jensen and Cowden had become members of the Board Committee and had some authority? Whatever the answers, the bulldozing was such an enormous affront in Daryl's mind that it obscured his grasp of the chronology of events. The bulldozing did ultimately become a symbol of destruction and loss for two generations of people since it meant there could never be any return. Yet, in spite of the bulldozing, the viewpoint of the blackfellas as expressed by Aunty Gina absolutely rejects victim-hood. Her story shows me that no longer can her family – the Kurnais – be depicted as the victims. They were resilient, agile, adaptive, wily; anything but victims.

I ask Aunty Gina if the move away from the Track turned out as she expected. I tell her that Hector Cowden thought it was a failure, that he was, according to his daughter, in despair about it. Aunty Gina expresses surprise at this:

> I don't understand why he thought our life at the highway was like
> that. The neighbours – the farmer up the road – they used to help us
> a lot. They were the Hornbys. We used to go get the milk off them,
> you know. And then we got to know a lot of people around Drouin.
> Men folk. They were good to us... They used to come to the place and
> all and they sat down to have a yarn and we would play the guitar
> and have a few beers. Everything was fine, I thought. You know we
> were all happy...

I tell her Jensen's comment about the overuse of alcohol and how that alarmed him.

Yeah, there was [alcohol] too. Yeah, I suppose they [Mr Jensen] seen some of that… In a way they did drink too much, but as long as they were at home drinking and not disturbing anyone… They always used to come up home… There used to be arguments, you know, but it was all over in a flash. The men might have a little punch up but then it was over. It was the men who were doing the drinking, not the women…

Here is a hint of the dissipation and depravity people like Councillor Stoll of the Buln Buln Shire Council were so frightened of, but Aunty Gina doesn't see it that way. In his memoir Daryl comments several times on the harm that drink can do. He declares himself a wowser and protests over and over that there was no alcoholism at the Track, but he never says there was no drink. As a matter of fact, he speaks fondly of a card game the boys had going on weekends as a way of winding down from hard work during the week. Gina seems to feel that this is how it was at the camp on the highway, as well. She passes over it lightly and continues:

Yeah, people say it was the best life… Our relations, they'd come for a visit. All those people who came would have been pea-picking. There was a farm out on South Road, there. He had peas and beans growing. That was seasonal work. They had their own tents… We lived in a hut and we built onto it. It was moved there. Built a veranda and a kitchen. Only a small water tank, but we had the pipeline running past… We used to drink the pipeline water, used to boil it before we drank it, but it tasted all right… Our houses were never filthy. They were clean. We never felt poor. We had plenty of food…

Aunty Gina's memories are nostalgic: she is trying very hard to put paid to comments directed at Aboriginal people about their squalor. Daryl also spent energy trying to establish a reputation for cleanliness on the part of his family, commenting many times that his wife Euphie was the cleanest woman he ever met. The preoccupation with cleanliness also comes from the inspections the Aboriginal women had to endure in their houses at Lake Tyers Mission Station, inspections that made them vulnerable to shame and ridicule. When Aunty Gina says they were clean and well-fed, I believe her. But, I am not so sure how comfortable they really were at the camp, for she says:

I don't know how long we were out at the highway. We were a long time until they moved us into town, but I wanted to move from the highway because the family was increasing and the little hut was too small. They moved me into Grant Street...

She pauses at this juncture, for all her memories of getting along well with White friends change when she and her family move into the town proper and face overt racism.

"I didn't have problems with whitefellas," Aunty Gina says. "They were friendly to us [but in town] we couldn't make a fire and sit around a camp when we got to Grant Street. Yeah, I wouldn't mind doing that again. But, yeah, when we moved into town, there were too many rules to follow."

"There were still these attitudes from some town people that blackfellas are no good," says Pauline. "People living in the towns had an attitude like they'd rather see a blackfella dead than see him walking around."

"Yeah," counters Aunty Gina, "I didn't feel that... I just stayed away from them fellas. Oh yes."

In the town Aboriginal customs and habits were scrutinised and brought into question; the people were expected to behave as Whites do. It was there that the assimilation idea fell apart, for neither group – the Aboriginal people nor the settler Australians – would change their ways for each other. Considering Councillor Stoll's reactions to the possibility of having Aboriginal neighbours, it must have been assumed by the townspeople that any accommodating should be entirely on the part of the Aboriginal people. But there is no indication from Aunty Gina or Pauline that they or their people wanted to change or were even aware that they had to change. In their minds since it was whitefella policies that put pressure on Aboriginal people to move into town, it made sense that any accommodating should have been done by Whites.

Daryl's story tells us what happened once the move into town proper took place: Aunty Gina does not want to remember those painful times. She pauses and then says, "I'd have loved to go back there [to Jackson's Track] because it was a beautiful place. Yeah, yeah, the kids were happy then, but..." The regret she expresses at leaving the Track is in retrospect. She was perfectly happy at the highway with family all around her. By taking all events and developments into account she can now say that life at the Track was a happy time. Later, when I go back over narratives by other members of the family, people who were children when the shift took place and who remember both the Track and the Camp, I see that they have a difficult time differentiating between the two places. It seems that they have mythologised both and their voices change tone to one of nostalgia when memories of life on either place leap into consciousness. Since Aunty Gina's family mingled freely with Euphie's family, the children missed each other when the move took place. Dot Mullett remembers being perfectly happy to go to Drouin to live at the Camp with her mother's sister when she started high school. She has many happy stories to tell about the antics she and her cousins got up to when they were kids. Murray Austin, who moved with his family to Neerim South, also spent time at the camp after the move. He tells humourous stories of his childhood with such enthusiasm that he loses his breath from laughing. I repeatedly interrupt him and Dot with, "Was this at the Track or the Camp?" for it is impossible to tell. Sometimes they can't remember even though they maintain throughout the interviews that the Track was a more special place than the Camp.[15] Does the Track seem more special because Daryl made it so with his memoir?

Dot Mullett
Photo by the author

At the time, none of the Aboriginal families had any idea of the scandal raging around them and their lifestyle. When I tell Aunty Gina about the things that were said in the newspaper articles, her reaction is to shrug it away as if it were none of her business.[16]

Diane Barwick says that many welfare workers and would-be reformers only pay attention to the so-called hard luck of Aboriginal people, but do not participate in the community's life sufficiently to understand its compensations of 'tolerance, compassion, humour, and emotional warmth of personal relationships [and of] complete acceptance of belonging by birth and by right, what ever their follies or failings, their status or successes'.[17] Daryl Tonkin had participated in this rich culture. No wonder he felt it as a tragic blow when his family left the Track. As a White and a landowner, he could not abandon his identity and leave it all to join his extended family. Having lost so much in his life, he found himself isolated in the bush and he chose to blame the do-gooders – Jensen, Buchanan and Cowden – for his grief. With my help, he painted a picture of the dispossession and victimisation of a powerless group.

As depicted by Aunty Gina, however, the move away from the Track was in essence an exchange between the do-gooders and the Aboriginal group. Stewart Hood must have decided to cooperate with Jensen and his cohort in order to get a lift for his family to the next destination. It was a reciprocal act: we will come to your church meetings, wear your hand-me-down clothes, sleep on your mattresses if you will find us a home closer to work. But as we can see from the accounts of both Jensen and Aunty Gina, once the move was made the cooperation was over. No matter how often the do-gooders visited the Camp, no matter how often officials from the Board or the Shire came to look them over and monitor their progress, the Aboriginal responses to these people remained coy and clever rather than open and truthful, and nothing would make them 'change their ways'. Was their refusal to assimilate an expression of their dignity and integrity? Or was it a reaction to a terrible betrayal?

Daryl felt betrayed by the do-gooders when his family left the Track. He thinks that if the huts had not been bulldozed, his people would have returned in a natural cycle of movement and all would have been well. It is possible that the Aboriginal people felt the bulldozing as a betrayal as well. Aunty Gina re-tells a story Daryl tells in his memoir about her father, Stewart, going out to camp at the Track regularly because he missed the old ways and needed to look the place over. Is the mythologising of the Track – as a place that allowed freedom of choice and independence – symptomatic of deep seated but controlled anger at how people like Jensen in unwitting collaboration with the Board tried to steal from them their ability to shape their lives by taking it upon themselves to eliminate their choices?

Aunty Gina's version of the story does not entirely clear up all the loose ends, but it gives a fresh point of view, forcing me to use my imagination in an attempt to see what she saw. She says that her life has been happy and full and, as I look at her, the central figure in this busy house, I see a woman who has lived her life practically and sensibly, with her extended family all around her. Aunty Gina, remembering her life selectively, has been untouchable. I can see her point of view. She never wanted to become a White person and she never did. The non-Aboriginal people trying to get her to assimilate or convert might call her intractable, recalcitrant, uncooperative, maybe congenitally stupid or lazy. They would be wrong. No matter how many conflicting pressures were brought to bear on her, Aunty Gina remained true to her customary allegiance to the group, the family whose members now number over three-hundred across Gippsland, all of whom call themselves Kurnai and defer to this old woman. Aunty Gina is what she is, a woman embedded in her own culture. There is no denying her culture is distinctive, no denying her Indigeneity.

Aunty Gina
Photo courtesy of the Rose family

After my long talk with Aunty Gina, I can look back to Pauline's speech on that Australia Day in 2000 with new eyes. I understand that she was revealing something true to all those old White settler Australians in the audience, sitting there amazed at how articulate, confident, and positive she was. While I'm sure that not many of them understood any better than I did exactly what she was saying, her independent and proud tone of voice rocked them to the core. They understood the importance of what she was saying, but only she knew the truth of it, and now so do I. She was telling us that her people and their culture are living, adapting and changing, that it takes alertness and agility of mind to understand this world and get along in it while maintaining integrity. She was telling us that in spite of all the good the whitefellas have tried to do to her and her people, in spite of their preconceived ideas of who she is, her sense of herself has never been entirely lost. It lives in people like Aunty Gina and now Pauline, along with the stories and laws. And so her people survive.

> It may seem as if the culture is returning to us, when actually it has never been lost, only hidden. The elders have made it their duty to guard our culture, like a hidden treasure, passing it down to a chosen few who would keep the stories. The storytellers were invested by the elders with our ancient memories and so they have never been lost.

ENDNOTES

[1] Pauline Mullett, 'Australia Day Speech', delivered at Drouin Australia Day Breakfast, 26 January 2000.

[2] Jan Critchett (1999) describes Collin Hood in *Untold stories; The memories and lives of Victorian Kooris* (pp. 95–106). Collin, described in the Warnambool *Standard* as 'a very intelligent blackfellow', was well known to bureaucrats – Alfred Deakin, Chief Secretary and Reverend Friedrich Hagenauer, Acting General Inspector of Aborigines – in that he was actively involved in the resistance to the closure of Framlingham. His story, that of dispossession and 'pulled down huts', very much parallels the story told by Tonkin, which happened sixty years later.

[3] This information is part of the 'map' that Aunty Gina holds in her possession. On the map Swan Reach is denoted as the place where the Kurnai clans – Brataualung, Tatungalung, Brayakaulung, Brabralung, as well as, Krauatungalung and Biduelli – came together for common ritual meetings.

[4] This research into ancestry was done for the Hoods by Jan Critchett (1999), some of which is included in her book *Untold stories; The memories and lives of Victorian Kooris*.

[5] Barwick (1981, p. 78).

[6] In her Doctoral thesis for Australian National University, Barwick (1963) says the Cumeragunja people who migrated to Melbourne after the 'Strike' in 1939 only use the word *blackfellow* in 'bitter and self-deprecating' jokes and that they use the word *Kuri*, meaning 'the dark people', in preference. This seems to have changed since 1963, or is quite different amongst Kurnai people. Aboriginal people in Gippsland refer to themselves as *blackfella* and avoid the word *Koori*, because, for the people at Lake Tyers, it is a word that was used to refer to invading tribal people who aligned with black trackers or native police working with Colonist settlers and caused grief for the Kurnai people. There are any number of oral sources to corroborate this: Aunty Mary Harrison, Paula O'Daire, Cora Gilson Waters, Alan West, Timothy Lee, Aunty Gina Rose, Pauline Mullett.

7   Barwick writes, 'Because they enjoy companionship and wish to repay past obligations, many dark people continue to live in large households shared with relatives. This continued sharing and foster-rearing of children maintain close ties among a large number of relatives and encourage adherence to common norms and values' (Barwick 1994, p. 28).

8   Interview with Aunty Gina Rose, Drouin, 24 March 2004. In this chapter, all direct quotations from Aunty Gina come from this interview.

9   Bain Attwood (1989 p. 61) cites a comment made by A. W. Howitt who knew the early Kurnai around 1880: '"There is a common obligation upon all to share food and to afford personal aid and succour." This "principal of community", he explained, was applied to Europeans and "the food, the clothes, the medical attendance which the Kurnai receive from the whites, they take in the accustomed manner"'.

10   B357/0 Drouin Wood Street Purchase; Letter from Aborigines Welfare Board to Housing Commission, 6 August 1958, from Aborigines Welfare Board to Housing Commission.

11   *Warragul Gazette*, 'Housing For Aborigines', 9 June 1959.

12   Beckett (1988, p. 195).

13   Landon, Carolyn. Notes from interview with Daryl Tonkin, 12 November 1997.

14   *Buln Buln Shire Council Minutes*, 30 September 1958.

15   Interviews with: Dot Mullett, Warragul, 20 April 2004; and Murray Austin, Drouin, 21 April 2004.

16   There is a series of newspaper articles in 1963 about the scandalous situation at the 'Camp on the Highway':

'Aboriginal Settlement Again Under Fire: Council Divided on Closure', *The Gippsland Independent*, 19 September 1963.

'Aboriginal Settlement Danger to Health', *The Gippsland Independent*, 20 June 1963.

'Cattle are cared for but Aborigines are not'. *The Gippsland Independent*, 15 August 1963.

'Drouin West Aborigines' Camp: "How do we stop them living there?"', *The Gippsland Independent*, 24 September 1963.

'Further Scathing Report by Local Medical Officer: Foul Conditions Still Exist at Aborigines' Camp', *The Gippsland Independent*, 10 October 1963.

'Letter to the Editor from Donald Thomson', *The Age*, 23 May 1963.

'Premier Being Asked to Close Aborigine Camp Near Drouin', *Warragul Gazette*, 28 October 1963.

And from 1964:

'Aboriginal Families Must Leave Huts', *The Age*, 21 April 1964.

17   Barwick (1994, p. 27–28).

REFERENCES

Attwood, Bain. 1989. *The making of the Aborigines*. Sydney: Allen & Unwin.

Barwick, Diane. 1963. 'A little more than kin: Regional affiliation and group identity among Aboriginal migrants in Melbourne'. Ph.D. thesis, Canberra: Australian National University.

Barwick, Diane. 1981. 'Writing Aboriginal history: Comments on a book and its reviewers, Australian National University'. *Canberra anthropology* 4 (2): 75.

Barwick, Diane. 1994. 'Aborigines of Victoria'. In *Being Black: Aboriginal cultures in 'settled' Australia*, edited by Keen, Ian. Canberra: Aboriginal Studies Press.

Beckett, Jeremy. 1988. *The past in the present; The present in the past: Constructing a national Aboriginality*. Canberra: Aboriginal Studies Press for the Australian Institute of Aboriginal Studies.

Critchett, Jan. 1999. *Untold stories, memories and lives of Victorian Kooris*. Melbourne: Melbourne University Press.

Cite this chapter as: Landon, Carolyn. 2006. 'Aunty Gina's story'. In *Jackson's Track revisited: History, remembrance and reconciliation*. Melbourne: Monash University ePress. pp. 7.1–7.19. DOI: 10.2104/jtr06007.

CHAPTER 8

THE BUSHMAN'S STORY: ONE LAST LOOK

Carolyn Landon

Constructing memory into a narrative is fraught with complexity as the teller is reassessing their life and creating a story of the past for the present. This final chapter explores the relationship of the interviewer and the testifier, asking questions about the influences, assumptions, and attitudes that existed when they first met and how these have changed in the face of new narratives that have been recently constructed about the same events. All of us who try to make sense of our memories and give meaning to our lives through story change the structure and emphasis of our accounts every time we tell them, depending on the context of the telling. If he could, Daryl Tonkin might tell his story differently now. As for those of us who are the listeners, it takes a great effort of imagination to pull our minds around to another's way of thinking so we can fathom and respect our sources. This epilogue speculates on the changes the listener and the teller might make to the initial story if they were to resume their collaboration.

If Daryl and I were to tell his story afresh, now that time has passed and other stories have been told, would it be very different from *Jackson's Track*? We would be better placed to discover the chronology of events, since the archive has been scoured, but I don't know if the facts and events he relates would change much. What might be different is the emphasis he gives them. And this would have as much to do with my ability to hear the meaning in his words as it would with any restructuring of his narrative.

What I can do now is look back at the book we wrote and see what I didn't see before. Yes, yes, it's all there: most of what Aunty Gina has said, a great deal of what Jensen has told me, much of what the Archive – especially the Historical Society – revealed. It's all there: for instance, the money owed to Daryl; the debt incurred at Pretty's store; the winding up of the business Harry and Daryl had been running; the cheating and drunkenness of Daryl's White employees left over from the time before Harry's death; the end of 'millable' wood on the property and the need to shift operations to the state forest and focus on fence posts instead of timber; and finally the people leaving the Track one at a time before the trucks came to take them away. Of course, they were leaving to find work, just as Aunty Gina said, not because they were afraid of the 'Welfare' and the Christians as I had heard Daryl say in our interviews. Had I heard him wrong? Had he been responding to my tastes? Was the emphasis we put in the book a combination of both of our needs? Were we so used to thinking of the family as Aborigines – those people who in the past have been seen as little more than victims of colonisation – that we could not see them as free-thinking, yet culturally bound, Kurnai who had reasons for what they did?

Even though he didn't take any notice of the official name of the Board or the existence of the League, Daryl knew something was going on that gave people authority to walk onto his property and drive people away to another place. He thought it was the Shire, but he didn't really care. I see now that I am the one who cared about officialdom oppressing the people at the Track and so perhaps it was my emphasis, my attempt to find a villain in the story, that made him name the Shire and let them take the blame for all the Leagues and Boards and Councils that might have done damage to Aboriginal people during the era of assimilation in every small town in south-eastern Australia. Was this – seeing the Hoods and Roses overwhelmed by a monolithic oppressor – the truth?

Daryl Tonkin
Photo by Julian Hills

Maybe, on at least one level, it was the truth. There seems to be nothing in the record that solves the mystery of who bulldozed the bark huts in which the Aboriginal people lived on Jackson's Track for twenty years or more. There is nothing in the Buln Buln Shire minutes from 1956 to 1964; nothing in all the correspondence between Davey,

Felton and Meagher. Yet, Daryl witnessed it; and no one would dispute his version for it has become part of the mythology of the Track. All who were involved there knew it happened, but no one except Daryl saw it happen. "I don't remember how I knew," said Alwyn Jensen. "I might have driven out there and seen it after it happened."[1] They all knew what it meant, too, just as Daryl did. Even Jensen understood the tragedy of that event. "It was final," he said, "because once they bulldozed, they had nothing..." The testimony of those who experienced events at Jackson's Track is what counts here since the record is silent. Daryl's account tells the truth in that it gives meaning to the event. Is this what made me hear his story one way and not another?

There are other things in his story I would hear differently now. I would hear a different meaning behind Daryl's labelling himself a *villain* and a *fool*. I can now go back to his book and see with different eyes the scene between him and Dora Hood, Euphie's mother, when she told him that he would have to be strong to face the racism that would raise its ugly head now he and Euphie had paired off. During her interview, Aunty Gina, after giving a quick conspiratorial glance at Pauline, said quietly, "Dora didn't like Euphie taking up with Daryl."[2] Of course! Dora's experience with White bosses may well have been fraught with negative feeling; after all, how many stories would she have heard of unknown White men who had loved and then left Aboriginal women? So, instead of giving Daryl advice, she might have been scolding him for what she thought was a wrong choice. As Stewart Hood's wife she may have been making an attempt to safeguard his/her lineage. Perhaps she was bringing up cultural issues in an attempt to protect herself and her people. Was it my interpretation or Daryl's telling that made us avoid such readings of that scene? Dora Hood would also have been concerned that Euphie and Daryl were breaking the law by being together, and Daryl would have known this when he told me this story. But I didn't ask him any questions which might have drawn out the true meaning of the scene. I went with my righteous outrage and Daryl was content to leave it at that. He was worried about repercussions then. Would he be now?

Would Daryl and I handle many of the events differently now? Yes, we would. We all change the structure and emphasis of our stories – those based on memories – every time we tell them, depending on the context of the telling. Our – his and my – understanding of the place of Aboriginal stories in our national history has changed a great deal in the ten years since we began working together. Bain Attwood summed it up in *The making of the Aborigines*: over the years, a Eurocentric view has given way to an Aboriginal view, which, in turn, has become a view of acculturation and accommodation between Aborigines and settler people. Close bonds of 'loyalty and affection' between

Daryl at home
Photo by Ingvar Kenne, © 2003

White and Black can now be readily recognised and we are willing to trace 'the rules and relationships of reciprocity concerning land and kin' as we have not been before.[3] I believe Daryl would be able to speak with much more candour and less shame now in 2006 than he did in the mid 1990s: telling his story helped him realise the changes that had been taking place over the years that he was silent about his life at Jackson's Track. I believe we would now be able to give the Aboriginal people in his story more credit for determining their own lives. In spite of these changes, it has been an effort for me to alter my suppositions about Daryl's story and about how Aboriginal people like Pauline and Aunty Gina see the world and respond to 'us', White settler Australians. It has taken an effort for me to do something so seemingly simple as listen to and hear Aunty Gina's story. In her Boyer lecture 'What We Make of Them' Inga Clendinnen introduces us to the work of the American philosopher Martha Nussbaum who believes it is imperative for us develop what she calls the 'narrative imagination', 'the ability to see unobvious connections between sequences of human actions and to recognise their likely consequences, intended and unintended'. Nussbaum says it takes a great effort of the imagination to pull our minds around to another's way of thinking so we can fathom and respect the 'other' that is before us.[4]

I think that at last we have put the Australian story of assimilation in a small corner of West Gippsland to bed. Even though there must be other connected stories that have not been told, the burden has been lifted. It seems to me that we have finally made room for the stories Pauline has to tell by tying up the old stories from the era of assimilation into a safe bundle, to be kept for posterity. Interested people can find out what happened here without ever again having to bear the burden of it as Daryl and his extended family have done. This must have been Pauline's purpose, all those years ago, when she came to me for help in finding out the 'true history of Jackson's Track'.

Courtesy of Museum Victoria: Registration No. XP 1651. Photographer: Richard Seeger

Jackson's Track
Photo reproduced with permission also from Regina Rose

ENDNOTES

1   Interview with Alwyn and Hilda Jensen, Neerim South, 8 April 2004.

2   Interview with Aunty Gina Rose and Pauline Mullett, Drouin, 24 March 2004.

3   Attwood (1989, p. 138).

4   Clendinnen (2000, p. 245). Nussbaum was talking about the Holocaust when she made these statements, but Clendinnen, like other historians and rights activists, sees a link between the lessons learned in the Holocaust and understanding Australian Aboriginal history.

REFERENCES

Attwood, Bain. 1989. *The making of the Aborigines*. Sydney: Allen & Unwin.

Clendinnen, Inga. 2000. 'What we make of them'. In *Essays on Australian reconciliation*, edited by Grattan, Michelle. Melbourne: Black Inc.

Cite this chapter as: Landon, Carolyn. 2006. 'The bushman's story: One last look'. In *Jackson's Track revisited: History, remembrance and reconciliation*. Melbourne: Monash University ePress. pp. 8.1–8.6. DOI: 10.2104/jtr06008.

BRABUWOOLOONG WOMAN

Carolyn Landon

In this epilogue, the story changes from one of History to one of Identity. Once the previous stories about the effect of assimilation policies on the Indigenous people of West Gippsland have been told, the weight of whitefella intervention into the lives of the Kurnai seems to lift. There is finally room for Pauline Mullett to begin her story. Now that Aunty Gina has set the scene, Pauline wants to talk about herself as a Brabuwooloong woman. She knows that the listener is finally ready to hear her words about country, family, culture and law. She knows the harsh reality is that her future, and that of her family, largely depends upon White Australians understanding who she is.

While I am still gathering the information for this book, Pauline, who understands better than I do the meaning of my endeavour, begins to tell me what she knows. She reveals for the first time that *she* has been given stories from her mother and Aunty Gina that will help inform the future for her people and for all of us. As I have said, until I spent time with Aunty Gina, I was not ready to hear Pauline's revelations. Now when Pauline tells me that the elders have kept much knowledge and they are passing it down, I am ready. I understand that because this knowledge is living in the mind, growing and changing yet being maintained generation after generation, the wisdom of someone like Aunty Gina has hardly been tapped by White Australians. Inside her must be a cornucopia of stories.

Inga Clendinnen talks of a cultural place where 'steepling thought structures – intellectual edifices'[1] keep traditions and truths intact through memory and ritual – story, song, sacred design and dance. Paul Carter says it is a simultaneous four [at least] dimensional knowledge.[2] Now that I have spoken with Aunty Gina I know that this cultural place exists in her, and now Pauline tells me that she too holds knowledge. All along Pauline has been challenging me to use my imagination to see through the darker water, as Inga Clendinnen puts it,[3] in order to understand the whole of a complex unfolding story. Until now I have been able to hear little more than guilty stories of wrong doing: stories of racial superiority, cultural incomprehension, baseless assumptions, unacknowledged cruelties, boundless ignorance and an absence of love.

At last Pauline has decided it is time to take me into the culture that she owns. She begins to tell me things I have never heard before, things about herself and her identity. Our talks together intensify. We meet for a quick coffee at one of the little places on the main street in Drouin and stay all day. Our conversations are animated, full of laughter, and sometimes anger and indignation, but mostly our words are in earnest. By getting to know me as well as she has, Pauline has been able to figure out through my reactions what we *gubbahs* don't know or comprehend and she alters her forms of expression to accommodate. Since talking to Aunty Gina, I can see clearly how much my understanding of Pauline has been a result of pre-constructed ideas of who she is. Now that I am tuned into this, Pauline works hard to deconstruct my Eurocentric mind-set and bring down the barriers between us. I concentrate and try to help her. As we stretch our imaginative faculties to encompass each other's worlds, we interrupt each other with expressions of new understanding or utter confusion. It is a reciprocal arrangement based on respect and friendship.

This is a long way from my first contact with Pauline in 1992 when I realised I needed help with the task of teaching her children. Pauline had only just started as Koori Educator then and was surprised at my request for help, but we hit it off immediately. After our first meeting I asked her if she would visit my classroom to teach Koori studies to the classmates of her children once a fortnight. She said yes, she had lots she could teach the students. But I remember that she also suddenly became coy.

"And there's lots more I could tell ya, but I won't," she said.

I wasn't sure what she meant, for I still believed then that most of the culture of Victorian indigenous people had been lost. "Why not?" I asked.

"Shame," she answered.

At the time her answer made me unbearably sad. I was also ashamed because it pinpointed my ignorance: it seemed to me that I must have blundered badly to force such an answer. Now when I remind her of that incident she laughs loudly. "A lot has changed since then," she says. Now I see that back then she had not meant, as I initially thought, that she was ashamed of her stories. She meant that there was no way I could have understood her, and so she wasn't going to try. She also might have thought it was not worth telling me because I would laugh and not believe her. I was not ready. She laughs now because I have come a long way.

I ask Pauline for a formal interview so I can use it in this project. Even before I ask her a question, before I can turn on the recorder, she begins talking. She wants to talk about Identity. Not so much about history anymore as Identity. This is the new story my project has been making way for: Identity. It is my place to listen. She slaps her open hand on her chest and says, "I am walking on the land. I am living. I am cultural history. I am the first person. I am the descendent of the people from here. My people have been walking for thousands of years on this particular bit of land."[4]

She shows me a description of her ancestors, living near Ninety Mile Beach, written in 1797 by Hugh Thompson, a mate on the ship *Sydney Cove*:

> We this day fell in with a party of native, about fourteen, all of them entirely naked... on this part of the coast [they] appear strong and muscular with heads rather large in proportion to their bodies. The flat nose, the broad thick lips, which distinguish the African, also prevail amongst the people on this coast. Their hair is long and straight, but they are wholly inattentive to it, either as to its cleanliness or in any respect. It serves them in lieu of a towel to wipe their hands as often as they are daubed in blubber or shark oil, which is their principal article of food. This frequent application of rancid grease to their heads and bodies renders their approach exceedingly offensive. Their ornaments consist chiefly of fish-bones or kangaroo teeth, fastened with gum or glue to the hair of the temples and on the forehead. A piece of reed or bone is also wore through the septum of the nose... Upon the whole, they present the most hideous and disgusting figures that savage life can possibly afford.[5]

Pauline is excited by this description of Kurnai men, which is a confirmation for her of their existence in her country before Europeans made maps, and she tells me how she feels a direct line from them to her. She thinks that since this description is made on paper by an old *wadjiman*, non-Aboriginals will see it as validating her own existence. I see something else and try to explain to her how the idea of the Aborigine was constructed in the mind of the European. When he describes the Kurnai people as hideous savages, Thompson, who in his own mind represents civilisation, is confronting not just 'untamed nature', but notionally the very beginnings of civilisation itself.[6] The Kurnai man then becomes the representative of the stone-age man in an ancient land meeting civilisation and progress in the exploring European man; for Thompson the one is doomed to give way to the other. For Thompson, the Kurnai is no longer a Kurnai, possibly not even human, but the symbol of an idea. This picture of an Aborigine has guided the definition of and management of Aboriginal people from the time of the invasion.

"Oh!" says Pauline. "For sure that Thompson didn't even know where he was or whose land he was on. Aw, gubbas know nothing!"[7] Pauline works hard to explain things to me. She articulates her ideas in her own fashion, struggling to find words. She finds it hard to realise that I don't know things about country, family, culture and law that she takes for granted as universal, but she struggles on. She knows it's important to try to speak her feelings because the harsh reality is that her future and that of her family depend upon whitefellas understanding who she is:

> My culture to me is Land. And anything on it to do with us. And spirit. Spirit is with the land. Spirit. Spirit can come in many forms. It can come in small signs of significance, you know, signs that... willy-wag-tail is a spirit form... and just signs of spiritual connection, the sun for instance... And it's also connected with the land. There is no spirit without the land. And we become the land... we become one with the land and its spirits.
>
> Oh, yeah, yeah, deadly, hey.
>
> It's a good feeling to know that you could have walked freely for centuries and in a tribal way... I mean we're a very common ground of people. I mean we were great warriors. Let me tell you, the Kurnai were the fierce ones and I believe that, too, you know, because Gippsland would have been very isolated from a lot of the other countries and our people were stern and strong, you know. So, I am very connected with my culture. I love it. And only because I discussed it... As I grew up, I learnt it more from Mum and her being a full-blood. It's because to me, black was beautiful, but her culture was passed on, and I didn't know who was related to who until she told me and she told us about the *dooligahs* and *nargans* and she was the one who told us about spiritual things coming in different forms. She talked about things generally that she's associated with her lifetime. And her Pop, her Pop would tell her what happened in his lifetime. Like, nobody today wouldn't know what a *nargan* was! People today wouldn't know if they saw a *dooligah* and you know they exist! They really do.
>
> I said to the parks and DNRE [Department of Natural Resources and Environment], "You people are destroying one of Australia's most ancient living artefacts walking around here!" And I meant the hairy things walking around here.

And they were looking at me and they're saying, "What do you mean? What do you mean?" you know.

And I said, "we called it the *dooligah* and you people are so out of tune with Aboriginal people and how they feel connected to their own land, you just don't understand."

They've got to put themselves in me to understand what it is like to be an Aboriginal. Only until you understand the history of this country and what we have suffered from...

As she continues to talk, I realise that she is taking me into her Archives. Unlike the huge monuments to ourselves we Europeans have built to enclose our histories, her archive is in the hearts and bodies of her people and in the country upon which they walk. We non-Aboriginals walk there too, but, as Pauline says, we don't know where we are and we don't see as she sees. Back in 1996 when I asked Daryl Tonkin what it was about Stewart Hood he most admired, he answered "His eyesight. He could see things in the bush minutes before I could... He could follow a track that I couldn't see and pick up the slightest clues as if by instinct."[8] I understood then that Daryl was speaking literally, but now I see he was also speaking figuratively. He was speaking of a place in the mind.

"Whitefellas call your history 'pre-history'," I say to Pauline, "because it's not recorded and so they find it very difficult to comprehend."

"Pre-history, my arse!" is her response, and then, as always, she laughs.

I give her a synopsis of what whitefellas think history is – that our history is about the record and how we interpret that record, and that the record is the written word. Greg Dening says the job of the historian is to re-text the texts.[9] "Whitefellas," I say, "find the traces of history – like you find it on the ground, and in the trees and with the birds and with the weather and the seasons and in your own identity, in your own self – on paper. And those traces go back thousands of years but there came a time when for historians those were the only traces that whitefellas counted."

"We [find] it in story telling, symbols and the land. The land tells the story," says Pauline. I understand that what she is saying is that Country is who she is, her identity and her history. The land tells the whole story – the first and the last story. What I hear her saying is that that is what makes it sacred. When we non-Aboriginals put our traces into buildings like the Archives they too become sacred places where anyone can go, but which only a few people know how to use. Her Archive is her country and anyone who knows how to see it, knows how to walk on it, will know who they are. When the Aboriginal people were moved from Jackson's Track to Comber's five acres on the highway, it was not so traumatic for them as it might have been – as I and perhaps Daryl assumed it was – for they were still in Country, and they still knew where they were and who they were. The Kurnai are people who, unlike many, have never been moved off Country. When Pauline says it is her life's work to walk her country and look out for traces of her identity, she means she is carrying on a tradition that has never been broken in Gippsland. I have travelled many places with her in her country and have listened to her tell stories about events or incidents that happened here and there. She points out landmarks of cultural and historical significance constantly. Wherever we are in Gippsland, as long as it is part of Kurnai Country, she knows where she is.

> I mean it's just... you feel it. There's a sense of... like I went to Tarwin Lower the other day and I just couldn't believe how I felt at home. I don't know, I just thought, 'Oh, I love South Gippsland. I just love it; I love driving along there...' Only because my grandfather is associated with Port Albert and the connection to Brataualong and he's... it's just the... only for my mother passing on those types of information we wouldn't know. That's what's maintaining and continuing the culture on.

It seems to me she is telling me that walking on Country still happens in south east Australia, that it is a continuing cultural habit that has not been broken. We have assumed that Aboriginal people stopped walking their Country by the end of the nineteenth century, but according to Pauline it still happens. The people who lived at Jackson's Track, but who came from different Country, often disappeared from the camp for days, weeks or months on end. Aunty Gina's husband Roy was often absent 'on business'. Pauline says he was walking his Country in the Western District. When Stewart Hood left the camp, Pauline, who described him as a strong, active, political man just like his father Collin,[10] believes he was walking Country: "Yes, Pop had this itchy foot, as they used to say, hey, where they've just got to go back into the country."[11] It seems that when Pauline takes me here and there, she is introducing me to her Country and showing me how to belong.

"I am a Brabuwooloong[12] woman," she says, "a clan of the Kurnai Tribe. I know my ancestors, Kitty Perry Johnson and Larry Johnson, and the lineage from them to me. This gives me the right, according to custom, to claim my identity and connection with

Country. I know the laws and customs and I have observed them all my life. They have been handed down to me from my mother and Aunty Gina. Now that my mother is gone, Aunty Gina is the elder. She holds the maps and designs in her possession. I am the messenger; I carry the message stick. Aunty could use the phone to ring people, but it is part of our tradition, shows more respect, if she sends a message through a messenger to the other elders. I am the messenger. I can't tell you any more, but I know all of it."

I ask her if she has read Howitt[13] for I wonder if that is how she knows the stories she is telling me. Bain Attwood talks about Alfred Howitt in *The making of the Aborigines*. He was hop farmer in Gippsland, who hired many Kurnai men to work for him, in particular a man named Tulaba, who allowed Howitt (at that point an amateur anthropologist) to record the Kurnai rituals and stories at a ceremony or *jeraeil* held at Lake Victoria in 1884. As a consequence, Attwood writes, 'the traditionally oriented [Kurnai] men and women did not effectively pass on their tribal law to the mission [Lake Tyers] Aborigines, but conveyed it instead to Howitt and so into European anthropological discourse (where it remained alienated from Aborigines until they recently began to seek the riddle of their identity in his ethnographic texts)'.[14] When Pauline says, yes, she has read Howitt, I ask her if she knew the stories before she read him. She answers, yes, she knew all of it and more.

"More?"

"Yes. From my mother."

"Can you tell me?"

She looks at me for a long time. Her expression shows that thoughts and feelings are streaking through her mind. I hold my breath. Have I got her over a barrel and are all the stories that are just now coming out about to retreat back to the dark?

"Spirits. They are about spirits... spiritual things. Mum told me. Aunty Gina knows. I know. I can't tell you. But I know things and I know who I am."[15]

And she keeps talking. Not for the first time in all this history of collecting the stories, I sigh a sigh of relief.

She tells me that the things in Howitt may not be entirely correct. She knows that Billy (Tulaba) McLeod's family now resides in New South Wales and that she is not entirely sure he is the Kurnai man Howitt thought he was. She says she knows that some of the people in the famous photograph of the *jeraeil* of 1884 are not Kurnai. She says that naturally, the men told Howitt only what the elders allowed them to, performed only those parts of ritual permitted to be seen by strangers.

"And it is only what the men told. Howitt only talked to men. The things I know are about women."

Of course! Once again we come up with that perennial problem of recorded history – androcentricity. "I know the things my mother handed down to me," Pauline continues. "In every family someone gets chosen to receive the law and the history. My mother told me things. Howitt never asked my female ancestors anything. But I still know what my ancestors knew even though he never recorded a thing."

Pauline sharing her stories
Photos by the author

Pauline is saying – once more, over and over, but I am listening now – that her ancestors did hand much of their knowledge down. Pauline insists it is still here. She no longer feels that she has to hide the fact that she has knowledge, and she now has the confidence to act on the authority that knowledge gives her. To me, this is an indication of how far the stories she wanted to hear, starting with those of her father, have taken her.

Pauline has often expressed concern that I, a migrant, have left my country: she has made it her business to introduce me to another. She explains that it is part of the Kurnai culture to accept strangers into their midst. Pauline's great grandfather, for instance, came into Kurnai country when he was quite old and met his new wife Helen, daughter of Kitty Perry Johnson, at Ramayuck Mission Station. Once he had married into the clan and accepted Kurnai as his country, he then had to abide by the customs therein and cast aside his identity as a Djab Wurrung man. Pauline seems to be acting on those principles with me: our friendship entails trust and loyalty. Of course, there is nothing formal about my introduction to her country, and so I have no responsibilities to carry out other than the responsibility I take on to never betray Pauline's trust. The responses of many other historians introduced to Country by their Aboriginal friends have been similar to mine. Peter Read reports that the historian Heather Goodall has deep connections with far north-west country in New South Wales after 25 years of profound engagement with Aboriginals there, particularly with her friend Isabel Flick.[16] For Goodall, as for me, the landscape is not enchanted, although she recognises that Country is mythologised and spiritualised for her Aboriginal friends. If Pauline and I drive past a *mrartchie* [spirit or ghost] place I can see her tighten up and feel the cold whereas I am left only to wonder. However, as Goodall says, she's felt "enough of the power of memory of places not to feel a need to [understand the spiritual]." She goes on, "I appreciate, but do not understand... I have an understanding of its emotional force. There is no single set of meanings. All of our understandings of the land are cultural."[17]

What I have understood about Pauline's country is that there are extra layers there to treasure, that her map is different from mine, that it is an ancient map of the mind that, begun as it was in deep history, is overlaid many times over with legendary events until it reaches the present. Jackson's Track is now a place on the Kurnai map that people travel to, where they can feel the spirit of the community that lived there. My map, until Pauline taught me to look differently, was roads and fences and towns. Now I have a strong sense of Pauline simultaneously holding herself in dimensions of past and present, and I can feel it too. Tom Griffiths feels, as I am beginning to under Pauline's guidance, that "awareness of environmental change and Aboriginality add to my sense of place... Aborigines and environment: these are the two great revolutions of our generation. Writing both into Australian history allows you to reach back beyond the moment of invasion and draws you into deep time as part of our own inheritance... Belonging to deep past implies nurturing deep future."[18]

Stuart Macintyre, in the introduction to his new *A concise history of Australia*, says that this new, finally recognised, Aboriginal presence confronts and challenges those of us who are trying to put our Australian story together.

> The idea of history as an unfolding of a necessary past no longer satisfies the imagination. The idea of Australian history as a story of national fulfilment succumbs to arguments of attachment and membership. The idea that this country has followed the path of the West... is challenged by alternative routes and destinations. The idea of an objective and universal record of the past exactly as it happened yields to myriad interpretations of a disposable past. The idea of the historian

as an impersonal, unselfconscious narrator is replaced by an appreciation of the historian who is present in the story. Time and memory are re-worked in the history that is now found to have commenced so much earlier. The traditional knowledge jostles with new discoveries to re-define beginnings.[19]

People like Macintyre, Griffiths, Goodall, Attwood, Reynolds, Read, Clendinnen, Beckett, and Sansom are at last talking with and listening to Aboriginal people, recognising their stories and understanding them.

To Pauline I would like to say this: "Through them and me you will at last be written into our Archive in your own voice, and we will be able to recognise you." But as I write this I think, why would this impress Pauline? Her archive is so much bigger and older than that of the whitefella. Perhaps also, containing spirits and myths and magic as it does, it is more complete.

It is the first story and the last story.

Pauline
Photo by the author

ENDNOTES

1   Clendinnen (1999, p. 59).

2   Carter (2004, p. xiv).

3   Clendinnen (1991, p. 275).

4   Conversation with Pauline Mullett, Drouin, 2 April 2004. All quotes from Pauline in this epilogue are from this conversation except where otherwise stated.

5   Austin (1974, pp. 20–21).

6   Beckett (1988, p. 194).

7   Conversation with Pauline Mullett, Drouin, 5 January 2005.

8   Landon and Tonkin (2000, p. 42).

9   Dening (1988, p. 2).

10 Stewart Hood along with Eugene Mobourne, both men from the Track, served on the Council for Aboriginal Rights to ensure Lake Tyers became an Aboriginal Trust. They believed the land was theirs as the place 'where previous generations had lived and died' (Attwood 2003, pp. 238, 240). Stewart's father, Collin Hood, worked with John Murray, MLA for Warnambool, to secure 500 acres of land for the exclusive use of Aboriginals (Critchett 1998, pp. 98–102).

11 Interview with Aunty Gina Rose and Pauline Mullett, Drouin, 24 March 2004.

12 All previous spellings of this word in the text have been based upon the spelling in A.W. Howitt. Now that Pauline is ready to tell her story, she wants to use the spelling that her Uncle William "Jock" Hood used when he named the five Kurnai Clans in the family map that he passed down to Euphemia, her mother. Pauline chooses to identify as Brabuwooloong, the clan of her ancester, Kitty Perry Johnson. Her great grandfather, Collin Hood, was Bratowoloong and other members of her family are Brayakoloong. The families in these three clans overlap according to her Uncle Jock.

13 Howitt (2001).

14 Attwood (1989, p. 79).

15 Conversation with Pauline Mullett, Drouin, 16 December 2004.

16 Flick and Goodall (2003, xvi): 'Isabel had known me a long time before she decided I could help her with her book. She had advised me in my earlier work in researching the history of Aboriginal people in their relations to land across New South Wales. She had also called me in to work on the documentation of the Aboriginal cemetery in Collarenebri...'

17 Heather Goodall speaking to Peter Read (Read 2000, p. 173).

18 Tom Griffiths speaking to Peter Read (Read 2000, p. 183).

19 Macintyre (1999, p. 5).

REFERENCES

Attwood, Bain. 1989. *The making of the Aborigines*. Sydney: Allen & Unwin.

Attwood, Bain. 2003. *Rights for Aborigines*. Sydney: Allen & Unwin.

Austin, K.A. 1974. *Matthew Flinders, on the Victorian coast, April-May 1802*. Melbourne: Cypress Books.

Beckett, Jeremy. 1988. *Past and present : The construction of Aboriginality*. Canberra: Aboriginal Studies Press.

Carter, Paul. 2004. *Papunya: A place made after the story*. Melbourne: Miegunyah Press.

Clendinnen, Inga. 1991. *Aztecs*. New York: Cambridge University Press.

Clendinnen, Inga. 1999. *True stories*. Sydney: ABC Books.

Critchett, Jan. 1998. *Untold stories : memories and lives of Victorian Kooris*. Melbourne: Melbourne University Press.

Dening, Greg. 1988. *History's anthropology: The death of William Gooch*. Maryland: University Press of America.

Flick, Isabel; Goodall, Heather. 2003. *Isabel Flick: The life story of a remarkable Aboriginal leader*. Sydney: Allen & Unwin.

Howitt, A.W. 2001. *The native tribes of south-east Australia*. Canberra: Aboriginal Studies Press. [originally published in 1904 by Macmillan]

Landon, Carolyn; Tonkin, Daryl. 2000. *Jackson's Track: Memoir of a dreamtime place*. Melbourne: Penguin.

Macintyre, Stuart. 1999. *A concise history of Australia*. Melbourne: Cambridge University Press.

Read, Peter. 2000. *Belonging: Australians, place and Aboriginal ownership*. Melbourne: Cambridge University Press.

Reynolds, Henry. 1990. *This whispering in our hearts*. Melbourne: Penguin.

Sansom, Basil. 2001. 'In the absence of vita as genre: The making of the Roy Kelly story'. In *Telling stories: Indigenous history and memory in Australia and New Zealand*, edited by Attwood, Bain; Magowan, Fiona. Sydney: Allen & Unwin.

Cite this chapter as: Landon, Carolyn. 2006. 'Brabuwooloong woman'. In *Jackson's Track revisited: History, remembrance and reconciliation*. Melbourne: Monash University ePress. pp. 9.1–9.12. DOI: 10.2104/jtr06009.

○ EXCERPTS FROM THE MCLEAN REPORT

EXCERPT ONE

CATEGORISING ABORIGINAL PEOPLE (PAGE 6)

Courtesy of the National Archives of Australia: B408, 10

Following is my report under the specific terms of reference. It will be noted that, throughout the report, where the terms " half-caste " and " aborigine " are used, they are to be taken as including all persons with an admixture of aboriginal blood, except where the more precise meaning is obvious :—

> (a) *The number, distribution, and living conditions of persons permanently resident in Victoria who are believed to be of not less than one-fourth part aboriginal blood, and the number of such persons who are—*
> > (i) *capable of working ;*
> > (ii) *regularly employed.*

To obtain this information, I enlisted the assistance of the police throughout the State, and, in respect of the metropolitan area, supplemented their figures with those obtained from other sources. The returns from all districts show that the total in the State, men, women, and children, is 1,346. Of this number, slightly more than half are children. It must be mentioned, however, that these figures, though as accurate as can be expected, are not statistically exact, particularly in terms of the heading. The principal inaccuracy arises from the difficulty of assessing the percentage of aboriginal blood in many cases. Over the succeeding generations, dating from the very early days of settlement till now, there has been such a high degree of miscegenation, and of sexual promiscuity on the part of aboriginal women and white men (and some coloured men of other nationalities), that such an assessment could, at best, be only approximate. Personal observation on my visits to aboriginal communities indicated that, included in the figures given, were some who were fairly obviously of less than one-fourth aboriginal blood, but who, brought up by their mothers in aboriginal communities, are generally regarded, by themselves and others, as aborigines. Though the figures given are subject to that qualification, this is perhaps not important, since they present the same problem, and are equally relevant to the purpose of this inquiry. The records of the Board show only about twenty persons, all adults, in Victoria as of full-blood, and the ancestry of some of these is at least open to doubt. Of 186 residents at Lake Tyers at the time of a survey made during this inquiry, 62 were shown as half-caste, 25 with a greater percentage of aboriginal blood, and 99 with less than half.

Of the 1,346 persons of aboriginal blood in Victoria, there are on an average about 131 at Lake Tyers station, and 159 in the metropolitan area. The remainder are scattered in various country districts, the majority in communities close to towns where seasonal work can be obtained, and to a river, on which they depend for their water supply. The largest individual group is in the Mooroopna-Shepparton area, where there are 253 regarded as permanent, of whom 162 are children. Large families are common among them, and there seems no doubt that the number of half-castes who are living in primitive conditions is steadily increasing.

EXCERPT TWO

THE 'CAPACITY' OF ABORIGINAL PEOPLE (PAGE 8)

Courtesy of the National Archives of Australia: B408, 10

> *(b) The capacity of people of aboriginal blood to live and maintain themselves and their families according to the general standards of the Victorian community.*

Though I make separate findings under this heading and the one next following, they are somewhat inter-related, since, in a wide sense, the present capacity of those of aboriginal blood to fend for themselves is influenced by existing factors, some of which may have a partial racial origin. With these factors I propose to deal under the next heading, and under this I interpret " capacity " as meaning " innate capacity ", and in that sense premise that the standard of any person's capacity to maintain himself and his family lies in his inherent physical and mental qualifications.

The physical capacity of the aborigines, taken as a whole, is undoubted. This is evidenced, if it were necessary, by their prowess in sports requiring a degree of endurance and skill, such as football and boxing ; and employers of aboriginal labour on seasonal work like fruit and bean picking, whom I interviewed, all seem to agree that in work of that nature they are frequently actually superior to the whites. Though many are prone to suffer from respiratory and other physical disorders, these are considered to be due solely to their living conditions from childhood, and to their habits.

As to their mental capacity, most authorities now agree that there is no innate racial inferiority of intelligence in the aborigine. In any case, there is a preponderance of white blood among those in Victoria, though some degree of degeneration from the general average of the white race might perhaps be expected from the fact that much of the white parentage has had its origin in the association of " sub-standard " whites, in an atmosphere of drink and degradation, with aboriginal women in their camps. I sought information from various sources on this subject. Close surveys have been made by Health, Mental Hygiene, and Education Departmental officers of the mental capacity of part-aboriginal children in various schools, and, though difficulty was experienced in applying the recognized intelligence tests, due to the children's timidity and suspicion, and their limited vocabulary, leading to some doubt as to the reliablity of the results, the general spread of those results was not markedly dissimilar to those expected of white children. I discussed this also with head teachers of long experience and careful observation in " mixed " schools, and with school inspectors. Some of the former furnished me with carefully tabulated records of individual children attending their schools, including some aboriginal children from better-class homes, and those bear out their opinion that, though the percentage of children of outstanding ability is higher among the whites, there is little difference in the general average of intelligence.

EXCERPT THREE

'OBSTACLES TO ABSORPTION' (PAGE 11)

Courtesy of the National Archives of Australia: B408, 10

Those obstacles to absorption which arise from the attitude of white citizens have their origin principally in racial and colour prejudice—the white man's notion of racial superiority—and in self-interest. The majority have a preconceived idea of the aborigine as sub-standard in every respect, and a readiness to regard the failings of many as common to all is perhaps understandable. This leads to a preference for white labour when it is available. Many white people have their failings as employees, but in most quarters have more chance of being tested on their merits than has an aborigine. I was informed by the Chief Employment Officer of the Commonwealth Employment Service that his service finds it very difficult to induce employers to take aborigines in certain jobs, the reason usually given being "because of their habits". There is also some degree of prejudice on the part of fellow-employees to aboriginal labour, though this is by no means general. Socially, it does exist, but this is largely attributable to difference in living conditions. I was, in fact, assured by two women of marked aboriginal descent, living in good working-class homes in two different country towns, that they and their children noticed no discrimination. Nevertheless, most will agree that mere colour-prejudice, on the part of some, does have a very real existence.

Some employers exploit the aborigines by under payment on seasonal work, such as fruit picking. When the latter, instead of complaining, leave for better remuneration, they are branded as "unreliable". Many, while the aborigines' services are gladly availed of for that urgent work, do not consider it necessary to provide accommodation for them, leaving them to shift for themselves and their families in improvised camps. When the work is finished, or is interrupted by weather conditions, they are regarded as nuisances by the general community, because of the habits for which its attitude towards them is partly responsible. These comments are, of course, by no means of universal application. Many employers do treat them as human beings, and in some places local committees and individuals, and bodies such as the "Save the Children Fund", do excellent work in their interest. However, in one place that I visited, where hundreds are employed in the season, and where their work is of considerable importance to the district, the only concern on the part of the townspeople in general, so far as I could discover, seemed to be that they should be kept out of the town, in the interest of "tidiness", and that someone else should do something about them. There is considerable scope for development among white citizens of more interest in the social problem, and appreciation of the need for conscious effort on their part to assist those of aboriginal blood to overcome their racial, educational, and temperamental disabilities.

EXCERPT FOUR

MCLEAN'S PROPOSED PROVISIONS FOR AN 'ABORIGINES WELFARE ACT' (PAGE 20)

Courtesy of the National Archives of Australia: B408, 10

As a means of bringing my recommendations and suggestions into effect, I finally recommend that an Aborigines Welfare Act be introduced, in substitution for the present Act, and that it include the following provisions :—

1. The term "aborigine" to be defined as including any person having an admixture of Australian aboriginal blood.

2. An "Aborigines Welfare Board" to be constituted, on the basis of my earlier recommendations.

3. The Board to be a body corporate, with the usual provisions applicable thereto, including the capacity to purchase, hold, dispose of, or otherwise deal with real and personal property, for the purposes of the Act.

4. All land now or in the future reserved for aboriginal purposes to be vested in the Board.

5. The Governor in Council to be empowered to appoint, subject to the Public Service Act, a Superintendent of Aborigines Welfare, and such other officers as may be necessary.

6. The duties and powers of the Board to be defined in wide terms, as follows :—

    (a) To, with the consent of the Minister, apportion, distribute, and apply as may seem most fitting, any moneys voted by Parliament, and any other funds or property in its possession or control, for the relief or benefit of aborigines, or for the purpose of assisting aborigines to become assimilated into the general life of the community.

    (b) Specifically, with the consent of the Minister, to acquire land, erect buildings, and sell or lease land, with any buildings thereon, to aborigines on such terms as it may determine.

    (c) To manage and regulate the use of reserves.

    (d) To exercise a general supervision and care over all aborigines, and over all matters affecting the interests and welfare of aborigines.

21

7. The Board to submit an annual report to the Minister, to be laid before Parliament.

8. The Board to have authority, subject to the consent of the Minister, to delegate powers to the Superintendent or other officers.

9. Re-enactment of Sections 11 and 12 (1) of the present Act, with the substitution in the latter sub-section of the words "the Board" for "a local guardian".

10. Averment in any legal proceedings by or on behalf of the Board that a person is an aborigine, to be sufficient evidence of the truth of such averment unless the contrary is shown.

11. The Governor in Council to be empowered to make regulations for the carrying into effect of the purposes of the Act, and in particular—

   (a) prescribing the mode of transacting the business and the duties generally of the Board and its officers.

   (b) prescribing the mode of distribution and expenditure of moneys granted by Parliament, and any other funds in the possession or control of the Board, for the relief or benefit of aborigines.

   (c) prescribing conditions of employment, other than payment, of aborigines.

   (d) providing for the control of reserves, including the maintenance of discipline and good order thereon, and the issue of licences to reside thereon.

   (e) imposing penalties not exceeding £20 for the breach of any regulation.

EXCERPT 5

EXCERPT FROM THE CONCLUSION OF THE MCLEAN REPORT (PAGE 21)

Courtesy of the National Archives of Australia: B408, 10

CONCLUSION.

In the foregoing report, I have, under the various terms of reference, endeavoured to present a picture of the "aboriginal problem" as it exists in Victoria, and have recommended that the Government should establish and maintain a system of administration much wider in its scope than hitherto. I have recommended that its concern should no longer be restricted to the welfare of those of aboriginal blood who have chosen to live in the sheltered environment of the station at Lake Tyers, and that, through a specially constituted Board, it should set in train an active and constructive policy directed to the social and economic uplift of the aborigines throughout the State, to the end that they may take their place in the ordinary life of the community. The implementing of those recommendations will involve some additional annual expenditure, but, if progress towards that ultimate goal is to take the place of retrogression, that is necessary. I emphasize again that, by its very nature, no early or spectacular termination of the problem can be expected, but I believe that a steady unremitting attack in the directions I have indicated will achieve definite results. It is inevitable that for many years to come there will be some aborigines who present no prospect of attaining to the general living standards of the community. It is perhaps also well to remember that, after many generations of civilization, there are white citizens in the community who present similar problems for society. It will be an important phase of the Board's activities to exercise supervision over the living conditions of those aborigines and their children, and for that purpose to establish close co-operation with civic authorities, health officers, and police, and, at the same time, to encourage and if necessary subsidize, local efforts directed towards improving the outlook of the rising generation.

I am convinced, however, that among the married couples of mixed aboriginal blood now living in sub-standard conditions, or on the station at Lake Tyers, there is at least a fair sprinkling who, given encouragement and assistance, would be prepared to make a real effort to establish themselves, with their children, in the community. As others marry, they will provide a field for the Board's special interest. The necessary encouragement to help themselves, and to persevere, can be imparted only by close personal contact, and that is an essential factor in my recommendations. Sympathetic treatment must be allied with firmness, their morale must be strengthened, and their readiness to accept the general concept of their inferiority removed.

○ PRIMARY SOURCES AND BIBLIOGRAPHY

Carolyn Landon

PRIMARY SOURCES

INTERVIEWS

Austin, Murray – interview: Drouin, 21 April 2004.

Jensen, Alwyn and Hilda – interview: Neerim South, 8 April 2004.

Mullett, Dot – interview: Warragul, 20 April 2004.

Mullett,Pauline – interview: Drouin, 2 April 2004.

Mullett, Pauline and Mobourne, Daryl – interview: Drouin, 31 May 2004.

Rose, Aunty Gina and Mullett, Pauline – interview: Drouin, 24 March 2004.

Cowden White, Flo – interview: Warragul, 22 April 2004.

NEWSPAPER ARTICLES

'Aboriginal Families Must Leave Huts', *The Age*, 21 April 1964.

'Aboriginal Settlement Again Under Fire: Council Divided on Closure', *The Gippsland Independent*, 19 September 1963.

'Aboriginal Settlement Danger to Health', *The Gippsland Independent*, 20 June 1963.

'Aborigines Sing at Warragul Meeting', *Warragul Gazette*, 26 August 1958.

'Aborigines to be Kept Out?', *Warragul Gazette*, 23 September 1958.

'Ashamed of our Treatment of Aborigines', *Warragul Gazette*, 22 July 1958.

'Cattle are cared for but Aborigines are not'. *The Gippsland Independent*, 15 August 1963.

'District League has Done Much to Advance Welfare for Aborigines', *Warragul Gazette*, 4 August 1959.

'Drouin West Aborigines' Camp: "How do we stop them living there?"', *The Gippsland Independent*, 24 September 1963.

'Further Scathing Report by Local Medical Officer: Foul Conditions Still Exist at Aborigines' Camp', *The Gippsland Independent*, 10 October 1963.

'Housing for Aborigines', *Warragul Gazette*, 9 June 1959.

'Keen Interest in Aborigines' Welfare in West Gippsland', *Warragul Gazette*, 19 August 1958.

'Letter to the Editor from Donald Thomson', *The Age*, 23 May 1963.

'New Home for Aborigines', *Warragul Gazette*, 2 August 1960.

'Plea for Better Deal for Aborigines', *Warragul Gazette*, 10 October 1957.

'Premier Being Asked to Close Aborigine Camp Near Drouin', *Warragul Gazette*, 28 October 1963.

'Report on Board of Inquiry', *The Age*, 1 February 1957.

'This Is What Our Readers Think: League's Protest', *Warragul Gazette*, 12 January 1960.

'Warragul Meets Leader of Expedition to Binidbu Tribe', *Warragul Gazette*, 15 July 1958.

'Welfare of Aborigines', *Warragul Gazette*, 18 March 1958.

ARCHIVAL MATERIAL

DOCUMENTS FROM THE NATIONAL ARCHIVES, VICTORIAN REGIONAL OFFICE

Aborigines Welfare Board: letter to Housing Commission. 6 August 1958, B357/0. Drouin Wood Street Purchase.

Chief Secretary's Department: Report signed by P.E. Felton, Regional Supervisor of Aborigines Welfare. 29 July 1958, B357 Box 5. Drouin Lease. Comber's Land. Princes Highway, Drouin East.

P. E. Felton: Letter to M. C. Taylor. 11 May 1962, B357/0 Box 5. Drouin 'camp' Princes Highway.

A. Jensen: Report to P. Felton. 19 August 1959, B357/0 Box 5. Drouin 'camp' Princes Highway 1958-64.

A. Jensen: Letter to J. H. Davey (Board Housing Member). 20 May 1959, B357/0 Box 5. Drouin 'camp' Princes Highway 1958-64.

McLean, Charles: Report Upon the Operation of the Aborigines Act 1928 and the Regulations and Order made Thereunder, Melbourne. 1957, B408. McLean Inquiry, Item, 10.

Report. 4 December 1958, B337. Housing – Drouin, Item 7.

Office of Chief Secretary of Vic, Hon, Rylah: Press Statement. 27 August 1962, B357/0 Box 5.

Superintendent Richards: Letter to Charles McLean. 23 April 1956, B408/0. McLean Inquiry: Police Reports & Population Details.

Victorian Aborigines Advancement League: Annual Report Concerning Camp. 25 June 1959, B357/0 Box 5. Drouin Camp Prices Highway 1958-64.

Warragul Gazette: extract. December 1960, B336 Box 3. 'Drouin and District Rates. Districts – Gippsland 1959-26'.

DOCUMENTS FROM THE PUBLIC RECORDS OFFICE VICTORIA, NORTH MELBOURNE

Buln Buln Shire Council Minutes, 30 September 1958.

OTHER

Jensen, Alwyn. *Report to NBAAL AGM 1967*, from the papers of Hector Cowden.
Jensen, Alwyn. Letter to Carolyn Landon, 22 February 2006.
Landon, Carolyn. Interview notes, 12 November 1997.
Mullet, Pauline. Australia Day Speech delivered at Drouin Australia Day Breakfast, 26 January 2000.
Mullett, Pauline. Talk delivered to Pembroke High School, August 2002.
Tonkin, Daryl. *The True History of Jackson's Track: Handwritten Manuscript*, Drouin, 1996.

BIBLIOGRAPHY

Anonymous. 1985. *Victims or victors? The story of the Victorian Aborigines Advancement League*. Melbourne: Hyland House Publishing.
Attwood, Bain; Burrage, Winifred; Burrage, Alan; Stokie, Elsie. 1994. *A life together, a life apart: A history of relations between Europeans and Aborigines*. Melbourne: Melbourne University Press.
Attwood, Bain. 1989. *The making of the Aborigines*. Sydney: Allen & Unwin.
Attwood, Bain. 2003. *Rights for Aborigines*. Sydney: Allen & Unwin.
Baker, Mark. 1997. *The fiftieth gate*. Melbourne: Harper Collins.
Barwick, Diane. 1963. 'A little more than kin: Regional affiliation and group identity among Aboriginal migrants in Melbourne'. Ph.D. thesis, Canberra: Australian National University.
Barwick, Diane. 1971. '20 changes in the Aboriginal population of Victoria, 1863–1966'. In *Aboriginal man and environment in Australia*, edited by Mulvaney, J.; Goss, J. Canberra: Australian National University Press.
Barwick, Diane. 1981. 'Writing Aboriginal history: Comments on a book and its reviewers, Australian National University'. *Canberra anthropology* 4 (2): 75.
Barwick, Diane. 1994. 'Aborigines of Victoria'. In *Being Black: Aboriginal cultures in 'settled' Australia*, edited by Keen, Ian. Canberra: Aboriginal Studies Press.
Beckett, Jeremy. 1988. *The past in the present, the present in the past: Constructing a national Aboriginality*. Canberra: Aboriginal Studies Press for the Australian Institute of Aboriginal Studies.

Cabral, Amilcar. 1993. 'National liberation and culture'. In *Colonial discourse and post colonial theory*, edited byWilliams, Patrick; Chrisman, Laura. Hartfordshire: Prentice Hall.

Clendinnen, Inga. 1991. *Aztecs*. New York: Cambridge University Press.

Clendinnen, Inga. 1999. *True stories*. Sydney: ABC Books.

Clendinnen, Inga. 2000. 'What we make of them'. In *Essays on Australian reconciliation*, edited by Grattan, Michelle. Melbourne: Black Inc.

Clendinnen, Inga. 2003. *Dancing with strangers*. Melbourne: Text Publishing.

Critchett, Jan. 1999. *Untold stories, memories and lives of Victorian Kooris*. Melbourne: Melbourne University Press.

Davey, Stan. 1963. 'Genesis or genocide? The Aboriginal assimilation policy'. *Provocative pamphlets 101* (July 1963). Available from: http://www.mun.ca/rels/restmov/texts/pp/PP101.HTM.

Deane, Sir William. 1996. 'Some signposts from Daguragu'. Inaugural Lingiari lecture delivered to the Council for Aboriginal Reconciliation, 22 August 1996. Darwin.

Dening, Greg. 1998. *History's anthropology*. ASAO Special Publication Number 2. Maryland: University Press of America.

Frisch, Michael. 1989. *Shared authority: Essays on the craft and meaning of oral and public history*. New York: University of New York.

Gaita, Raimond. 1999. *A common humanity*. Melbourne: Text Publishing.

Garner,Helen. 2004. *Joe Cinque's consolation*. Sydney: Pan Macmillan.

Goodall, Heather. 1996. *Invasion to embassy: Land in Aboriginal politics in New South Wales, 1770–1972*. Sydney, Australia: Allen & Unwin.

Howitt, A. W. 2001. *The native tribes of South-East Australia*, facsimile edition of book first published in 1904. Canberra: Aboriginal Studies Press.

Jackomos, Alick; Fowell, Derek. 1991. *Living Aboriginal history of Victoria: Stories in the oral tradition*. Melbourne: Museum of Victoria Aboriginal Cultural Heritage Advisory Committee, Cambridge University Press.

Kerin, Sitarani. 1999. *An attitude of respect: Anna Vroland and Aboriginal rights, 1947–1957*. Melbourne: Monash Publications in History.

Landon, Carolyn; Tonkin, Daryl. 1999. *Jackson's Track: Memoir of a Dreamtime place*. Melbourne: Penguin.

de Lepervauche, Marie; Bottonley, Gillain, editors. 1998. *The cultural construction of racism. Sydney Studies in Society and Culture*. Sydney: University of Sydney Press.

MacFarlane, Ian. 1993. 'Glimpses from the past'. In *My heart is breaking: A joint guide to the records about Aboriginal people in the Public Records Office of Victoria and the Australian Archives, Victorian Regional Office*. Canberra: Australian Government Publishing Service.

Macintyre, Stuart. 1999. *A concise history of Australia*. Melbourne: Cambridge University Press.

Manning, Corinne 2002. 'The McLean report: Legitimising Victoria's new assimilationism'. *Aboriginal history* 26: 159–176.

Murphy, John. 1986. 'The voice of memory: History, autobiography and oral memory'. *Historical studies* 22 (87): 157–175.

Nafisi, Azar. 2003. *Reading Lolita in Tehran*. New York: Random House.

Pepper, Phillip; De Aruago, Tess. 1985. *The Kurnai of Gippsland*. Melbourne: Hyland House Publishing.

Perks, R.; Thomson, A. 1998. 'Introduction'. In *The oral history reader*. London: Routledge.

Read, Peter. 2000. *Belonging: Australians, place and Aboriginal ownership*. Melbourne: Cambridge University Press.

Reynolds, Henry. 1990. *This whispering in our hearts*. Melbourne: Penguin.

Russell, Lynette. 2000. *Savage imaginings: Historical and contemporary constructions of Australian Aboriginalities*. Melbourne: Australian Scholarly Publishing.

Sansom, Basil. 2001. 'In the absence of vita as genre: The making of the Roy Kelly story'. In *Telling stories: Indigenous history and memory in Australia and New Zealand*, edited by Attwood, Bain; Magowan, Fiona. Sydney: Allen & Unwin.

Stanner, W. E. H. 1968. *After the Dreaming*. Sydney: ABC Books.

Steedman, Carolyn. 2001. *Dust*. Manchester: Manchester University Press.

Thomson, Alastair. 1994. *Anzac memories: Memory and wartime bereavement in Australia*. Melbourne: Melbourne University Press.

Watson, Don. 1984. *Caledonia Australis: Scottish highlanders on the frontier of Australia*. Sydney: Collins.

Watson, Don. 2002. *Recollections of a bleeding heart: Portrait of Paul Keating PM*. Sydney: Random House.

Whitlam, Gough. 1985. *The Whitlam government 1972–1975*. Melbourne: Viking Press.

Wurm, S. A. 1963. *Some remarks on the role of language in the assimilation of Australian Aborigines*. Canberra: Linguistic Circle of Canberra Publications.

Published by Monash University Publishing
Matheson Library Annexe, Monash University
Clayton, VIC 3800
Australia
https://publishing.monash.edu/

First published 2006

Cover photograph courtesy of Museum Victoria: Registration No. XP 1565.
Photographer: Richard Seeger. Reproduced with permission of Regina Rose.
Cover design: Les Thomas
Internal design: A. Katsionis

ISBN 978-0-9757475-7-5 (paperback)
ISBN 978-0-9757475-6-8 (ebook)

○ ABOUT THE AUTHOR

Carolyn Landon is co-author, with Daryl Tonkin, of *Jackson's Track: Memoir of a Dreamtime Place* (Penguin, Australia, 2000) and *Cups with No Handles: Memoir of a Grassroots Activist* (Hybrid Publishers, Australia, 2008), a biography of Bette Boyanton. Born in the USA, Landon came to Australia in 1968 as a traveller, hitchhiking by small aeroplane throughout the far north. A teacher in Australian state schools for almost thirty years, she has written and published several musical plays with her husband, Larry Hills. Landon has a masters degree in biography and life writing from Monash University.